Praise for *Syntactic Analysis*

"An excellent, original introduction, which treats linguistics as a science and language as an object of rigorous inquiry. Sobin succeeds in making the material user-friendly without simplification, and in engaging the reader in formulating and testing hypotheses about linguistic structures. A welcome addition to the growing body of books on the nature of linguistic inquiry and analysis."

Maria Polinsky, Harvard

"This book is a breath of fresh air. Any reader who wants an accessible introduction to what has been blowing in the wind will do no better than begin here."

Samuel Jay Keyser, MIT

"*Syntactic Analysis* is unusual among the introductory syntax texts on offer: it is more concise than most of them, yet covers an astounding number of topics in depth and detail. This should be the perfect introductory syntax text for upper-class linguistics majors and minors, and for MA students in linguistics- an audience for whom most existing texts may be too detailed and cumbersome. The exercises make this book particularly valuable."

Jaklin Kornfilt, Syracuse University

Syntactic Analysis

The Basics

Nicholas Sobin

A John Wiley & Sons, Ltd., Publication

This edition first published 2011
© 2011 Nicholas Sobin

Blackwell Publishing was acquired by John Wiley & Sons in February 2007. Blackwell's publishing program has been merged with Wiley's global Scientific, Technical, and Medical business to form Wiley-Blackwell.

Registered Office
John Wiley & Sons, Ltd, The Atrium, Southern Gate, Chichester, West Sussex, PO19 8SQ, United Kingdom

Editorial Offices
350 Main Street, Malden, MA 02148-5020, USA

9600 Garsington Road, Oxford, OX4 2DQ, UK

The Atrium, Southern Gate, Chichester, West Sussex, P019 8SQ, UK

For details of our global editorial offices, for customer services, and for information about how to apply for permission to reuse the copyright material in this book please see our website at www.wiley.com/wiley-blackwell.

The right of Nicholas Sobin to be identified as the author of this work has been asserted in accordance with the UK Copyright, Designs and Patents Act 1988.

Wiley also publishes its books in a variety of electronic formats. Some content that appears in print may not be available in electronic books.

Designations used by companies to distinguish their products are often claimed as trademarks. All brand names and product names used in this book are trade names, service marks, trademarks or registered trademarks of their respective owners. The publisher is not associated with any product or vendor mentioned in this book. This publication is designed to provide accurate and authoritative information in regard to the subject matter covered. It is sold on the understanding that the publisher is not engaged in rendering professional services. If professional advice or other expert assistance is required, the services of a competent professional should be sought.

Library of Congress Cataloging-in-Publication Data

Sobin, Nicholas.
  Syntactic analysis / Nicholas Sobin.
      p. cm.
  Includes bibliographical references and index.
  ISBN 978-1-4443-3895-9 (alk. paper) – ISBN 978-1-4443-3507-1 (pbk. : alk. paper)
  1. Grammar, Comparative and general–Syntax.   2. Linguistic analysis (Linguistics)
I. Title.
  P291.S546 2010
  415–dc22

                                                                                    2010029414

A catalogue record for this book is available from the British Library.

Set in 10/12 pt Sabon by Thomson Digital, Noida, India.

Printed in the UK

Contents

This chapter introduces hypothesis formation and testing in the realm of human language and discusses the paradox of language acquisition. It offers an initial sketch of the Principles & Parameters approach and the innateness hypothesis.

Words are analyzed into roots and affixes. A system of generative word formation is introduced involving morphemes and word formation rules. Also discussed are criteria for identifying the lexical class of roots, stems, and words. Finally, a discussion of the "meaning" of particular affixes leads to the conclusion that affixes do not have "simple" meanings, but instead participate with a constellation of other factors to determine meaning, something referred to as "compositional" semantics.

Tests of phrasehood are introduced, indicating the presence of hierarchic structure within sentences. Also presented is some of the core terminology of syntactic relations among phrases.

4   Rules of Sentence Structure: A First Approximation   38

Phrase structure rules are introduced as a means of explaining the presence of hierarchic structure within sentences. Beyond basic phrasal structure, key concepts such as structural ambiguity and recursion are presented as further evidence of the efficacy of the phrase structure approach to the analysis of sentences. Recursion is noted as the key to explaining "linguistic creativity."

5   Assigning Meaning in Sentences   53

Presented here is the system of determining grammatical function (subject, object, or adjunct) based on structural position. Building on this, theta roles and argument structure are introduced, offering an explanation both of how arguments (subjects, objects, etc.) get their explicit meanings, and how verbs "choose" the correct complementation pattern.

6   Some Category-Neutral Processes   63

Here, the notion of "category-neutral" processes is first introduced, paving the way for the generally category-neutral system of X-bar syntax presented later. The processes discussed here are coordination and proform insertion.

7   How Structure Affects Pronoun Reference   71

This chapter introduces c-command and some of the phenomena that c-command has been crucial for explaining, including the distribution of negative polarity items, and the Binding Principles, the distribution and semantics of anaphors and pronominals, and referring expressions. The presence of such mechanisms as the Binding Principles in the theory of syntax points offers further support for the innateness hypothesis.

8   Complex Verb Forms   82

The case is made here that auxiliary verbs each head a VP, so that sentences with multiple verbs involve a recursive VP architecture. Also, the first transformation, Affix Hopping, is introduced, opening the discussion of transformational grammar, and the levels deep structure and surface structure.

9 Real vs. Apparent Sentence Structure 90

Tense affixes are argued here to originate in the same position as modal verbs do, leading to the claim that deep structure is "abstract," that is, consistently different in its alignment of elements from that seen in surface forms. Also discussed is the position of negation and the head movement rule V-to-T, which raises an auxiliary verb to the position of tense. All of this expands the transformational view of syntax. Arguments are presented for the presence of a "null" tense affix in sentences like "They like beans," making the system of affixation fully general.

10 Generalizing Syntactic Rules 104

Arguments are advanced that phrases headed by the major lexical categories NP, VP, AjP, and PP share the same internal architecture, pointing toward the conclusion that the rules of the syntactic system are category-neutral rather than category-specific – instead of having separate rules for NP or VP, a single, general rule set explains the internal architecture of all major phrase types.

11 Functional Categories 116

The category-neutral analysis is extended here to functional categories such as T and C, leading to the conclusion that the system of syntax is completely category-neutral. The rules of syntax are few and simple. The specific details of derivations are largely driven by the features and argument structure of the words/morphemes employed in the derivation. The concept of parameter setting is developed further.

12 Questions, Relative Clauses, and *WH* Movement 127

A number of apparent anomalies raised in the detailed consideration of *WH* questions and relative clauses are resolved by addition of the transformation "*WH* movement." *WH* movement exemplifies phrase movement to a non-argument position. Apparent "long" *WH* movement is shown to be composed of series of "short" moves. The *WH* Island Effect is introduced in connection with this discussion. The syntactic system is argued to be "constructionless", since its rules apply broadly, across different construction types.

Arguments are advanced for the VP-internal subject hypothesis, the idea that the subject of a sentence originates low, in SpecVP, rather than in its higher surface position, SpecTP. This indicates the existence of a rule, NP movement, which searches for an NP low in the structure to fill the SpecTP position. This leads easily into the analysis of passive sentences, where no subject appears in SpecVP (due to theta role suppression), so that Move NP must find another (non-subject) argument to fill the SpecTP position. NP movement is also central to explaining subject-to-subject-raising constructions, where a higher clause may "steal" the subject of a lower clause. Like *WH* movement, NP movement participates in deriving a range of constructions, supporting further the view that the syntactic system is both category-neutral and construction-neutral.

Here, three further significant aspects of syntactic analysis are sketched out, anticipating further studies in syntax. These include the unaccusative hypothesis (the idea that the subject of certain apparently intransitive verbs actually starts as an object), the VP shell hypothesis (the idea that multiple complements are not "flat" but involve asymmetrical c-command), and the DP hypothesis (the theory that "traditional" NPs are in fact DPs, phrases headed by the functional category D).

Acknowledgments

I am indebted to a great many people for quite a variety of contributions which directly or indirectly, short-term or long-term, influenced the creation of this book. Central among these are Jon Amastae, Emmon Bach, C. L. Baker, Bob Borsley, Noam Chomsky, Ellen Courtney, Michel DeGraff, Joyce Fleur, Robert T. Harms, C.-T. James Huang, Sabine Iatridou, Yuki Ike-uchi, Lauri Karttunen, S. Jay Keyser, Jaklin Kornfilt, Susumu Kuno, Howard Lasnik, Marvin Loflin, Howell McCullough, David Pesetsky, Stan Peters, Masha Polinsky, Andy Rogers, Carlota S. Smith, and Arnold Zwicky. I also owe a huge debt of thanks to the many linguistics students at Texas, Pan American, Iowa, UALR, University of Wales-Bangor, and UTEP whom it has been my privilege to work with over the years.

Many thanks also to the Department of Linguistics at Harvard University and the Department of Linguistics & Philosophy at MIT each for hosting me as a Visiting Scholar on a number of occasions. My life in linguistics has been much richer for these experiences.

I'd like to offer special thanks to the editors at Wiley-Blackwell Danielle Descoteaux, Julia Kirk, and Anna Oxbury for their consistent encouragement and professional guidance on this project.

To my parents Edith and Ray, and my sisters Sue and Tina, my thanks for all their support in my (and our) academic endeavors. None of us would be where we are without it.

This work is dedicated to AnneMarie Sobin, gardener, fiction writer, and bricklayer, with thanks for the use of her superb copy editing skills, and for encouraging and supporting nearly everything I've wanted to attempt, some of which actually worked.

Abbreviations

$-\emptyset_{pres}$	"zero" present tense verb suffix
A (movement)	(movement to) an argument position
A′ (movement)	(movement to) a non-argument position
A-position	an argument position
A′-position	a non-argument position (e.g. Spec)
acc	accusative case
AH	Affix Hopping
Aj	adjective
AjP	adjective phrase
Arg	argument
Aux	auxiliary verb
Av	adverb
AvP	adverb phrase
C	complementizer (functional head)
c-command	constituent command
Cat	syntactic category
C_{HL}	computational system for human language (the subconscious grammar)
Comp	complementizer (early characterization)
Conj	conjunction
CP	complementized phrase
D	determiner (article)
DP	determiner phrase
D-str	deep structure
$-ed_{pst}$	"past tense" verb suffix
$-ed/en_{pstprt}$	"past participle" verb suffix
$-er_{compr}$	"comparative" adjective or adverb suffix
$-est_{sprl}$	"superlative" adjective or adverb suffix
exper	the theta role "experiencer"

FCH	functional category hypothesis
fin	finite
GF	grammatical function
-ing$_{\text{presprt}}$	"present participle" verb suffix
infin	infinitival
Int	intensifier
M	modal verb
N	noun
N′	N-bar
Neg	negative (functional head)
NegP	negative phrase
nom	nominative case
NP	noun phrase
NPI	negative polarity item
P	preposition
PossP	possessive phrase
PP	prepositional phrase
ProAjP	pro-adjective phrase
ProN′	pro-N-bar
ProNP	pro-noun phrase
ProPP	pro-prepositional phrase
ProV′	pro-V-bar
ProVP	pro-verb phrase
ProXP	variable ranging over proforms
PS (grammar)	phrase structure (grammar)
Quan	quantifier (in VP)
[−Q]	declarative feature on C
[+Q]	interrogative feature on C triggering T-to-C
R-expression	referring expression
S	sentence
SAI	Subject-Auxiliary Inversion
spec	specifier
-s$_{\text{pl}}$	"plural" noun suffix
-s$_{\text{pres-3rd-sg}}$	"third-person singular present tense" verb suffix
S-str	surface structure
T	tense (functional head)
TP	tense phrase
T-to-C (Movement)	tense-to-complementizer (movement)
UG	Universal Grammar
V	verb
V′	V-bar

VP	verb phrase
V-to-T (Movement)	verb-to-tense (movement)
WH movement	movement of a *wh* phrase to SpecCP
WHQ	*wh* question, a question containing a *wh* phrase
X	variable ranging over any syntactic category
XP	variable ranging over any phrasal category
YNQ	yes/no question

Introductory Notes and References

Introduction

What is going on in the mind of a three-year-old? A young human child, who can't yet learn to add 2 and 2 or to tie its shoe, is putting together in her/his head the grammar of the surrounding language. This is an astounding feat, as evidenced in part by the fact that linguists (scientists who study language) have yet to fully understand how any such grammatical system works or precisely what it contains. By around the age of 5, this child will possess a very sophisticated adult-compatible version of the language. This fact is tacitly recognized in many cultures that only let children begin formal schooling at around that age. The main requirement for such schooling is that the child be able to speak the language well enough to talk to and understand an adult stranger, namely the teacher. So around the age of 3, children are in the midst of developing the grammar of their language (or languages, in multilingual settings).

   To make the question above somewhat more specific, what we are asking is this: What does the child learn when (s)he learns a human language? If we define a language as the set of all of the sentences that are possible (i.e. German is all that stuff that sounds like German, etc.), then the fact that there is no "longest" sentence in a human language clearly indicates that the language (the set of possible sentences) is infinitely large and could not be "memorized" or learned directly. So instead, the child must be creating a "grammar" (the traditional term used above), or better, a computational system, a system that lets the speaker "compute" any of the infinitely many possible sentences of the language. In essence, when we study and do research in linguistics, what we are trying to discover are the particulars of this computing system. What are its basic elements, and what are the rules of their combination into the things that we call sentences?

Purpose

This book is intended as a brief introduction to modern generative syntax in the Chomskyan tradition. There are many fine introductions to this subject that are more lengthy and detailed. The purpose of this shorter text is to offer in a highly readable style an amount of information and accompanying work that is significant, but that also can be covered at a reasonable pace in a quarter or trimester format, or in half of a full semester, where the other half might deal with other aspects of linguistic analysis, readings in linguistics, or competing theories. Though brief, this work nonetheless has the goals of (1) introducing the reader to terms and concepts that are core to the field of syntax; (2) teaching the reader to understand and operate various syntactic analyses, an essential aspect of hypothesis formation and testing; (3) offering the reader the reasoning behind the choice of one analysis over another, thus grounding the reader in linguistic argumentation; and (4) preparing the reader for more advanced study of/research into syntactic systems.

No introductory work offers or can offer a complete picture of the field, but the topics dealt with here are central to the study of syntax. They form a coherent set that will serve the purpose of facilitating more in-depth study and research. As many have come to realize, this is one of the most fascinating areas in the study of human cognition.

Chapter Notes

This text deals with various areas of syntactic analysis that are fundamental to formulating modern theories of syntax. Rather than giving many elaborated references to current work, I will focus here on citing works that were foundational to the analyses discussed in this book, or that offer broad insight into them. The discussion of language acquisition in Chapter 1 is based on observations noted in Slobin (1979), and those of Chomsky (1999). In Chapter 2, some of the traditional grammar characterizations are those of Fowler (1983). The initial linguistic criteria for establishing lexical class membership is elaborated in Stageberg (1981). Katamba (1993) offers a detailed account of the generative approach to morphology. Finally, Vendler (1967) is a foundational work on compositional semantics. In Chapters 3 and 4, the full import of tests of phrase structure as implying the possible existence of rules of phrase structure was first established in Chomsky (1957) and extended in Chomsky (1965). The core notions in Chapter 5 that grammatical functions may be structure-based and are key to assigning theta roles are due to Chomsky (1981). These evolve into the theory of argument structure, developed in Grimshaw (1990). Coordination, as discussed in Chapter 6, was cited by Chomsky (1957: 35) as possibly "one of the most productive processes for forming new sentences…" suggesting its category-neutral character. In Chapter 7, the notions of c-command relation and Binding Theory were pioneered in the works of Reinhart (1976; 1981; 1983), in Chomsky (1981), and more recently in Grodzinsky and Reinhart (1993). The "phrasal Aux" hypothesis in Chapter 8 is from Chomsky (1957), and the "recursive VP" analysis of auxiliary verbs is based on Ross (1969). Affix Hopping is originally due to Chomsky (1957). The notions of transformation, deep structure, and surface structure were pioneered in Chomsky (1957). In Chapter 9, the analysis of tense affixes as independent syntactic elements originated in Chomsky (1957). The foundational work on "head movement" (movement of a head to another head position such as "V-to-T", and later "T-to-C") is that of Travis (1984). In Chapters 10 and 11, the foundational work leading to the general theory of category-neutral X-bar syntax was that of Chomsky (1970) and Jackendoff (1977). The Principles & Parameters approach to language acquisition and syntactic analysis was pioneered by Chomsky (1981) and Chomsky and Lasnik (1983), with key data contributed by Greenberg (1966). In Chapters 12 and 13, the transformational analysis of interrogative and passive sentences was first broached by Chomsky (1957), and has evolved through nearly all of his works (and of course those of many others) since. Most influential in recent times has been the "constructionless" view of transformation, as articulated in Chomsky (1981) onward. Bresnan's (1970) analysis of complementizers in interrogatives also provided some crucial analytic keys to the analysis of interrogatives. Emonds' structure-preserving hypothesis (1970; 1976) also represents a milestone in the analysis of NP movement. The work on syntactic "islands" was pioneered by Ross (1967). The VP-internal subject hypothesis originated in Koopman and Sportiche (1991). In Chapter 14, Perlmutter (1978) formulated the unaccusative hypothesis, Larson (1988) advanced the VP shell hypothesis, and Abney (1987) and Longobardi (1994) evolved the DP hypothesis.

References

Abney, Steve. 1987. The English noun phrase and its sentential aspect. Ph.D. dissertation, MIT, Cambridge, MA.

Bresnan, Joan. 1970. On complementizers: towards a syntactic theory of complement types. *Foundations of Language* 6: 297–321.

Chomsky, Noam. 1957. *Syntactic Structures*. The Hague: Mouton.

Chomsky, Noam. 1965. *Aspects of the Theory of Syntax*. Cambridge, MA: MIT Press.

Chomsky, Noam. 1970. Remarks on Nominalization. In R. Jacobs and P. Rosenbaum (eds.), *Readings in English Transformational Grammar*. Waltham, MA: Ginn, 184–221.

Chomsky, Noam. 1981. *Lectures on Government and Binding*. Dordrecht: Foris.

Chomsky, Noam. 1986. *Barriers*. Cambridge, MA: MIT Press.

Chomsky, Noam. 1995. *The Minimalist Program*. Cambridge, MA: MIT Press.

Chomsky, Noam. 1999. An interview on Minimalism. Ms., University of Siena, Italy.

Chomsky, Noam, and Howard Lasnik. 1993. Principles and parameters theory. In J. Jacobs, A. van Stechow, W. Sternfeld, and T. Vennemann (eds.), *Syntax: An International Handbook of Contemporary Research*, Berlin: de Gruyter, 505–69.

Emonds, Joseph. 1970. Root- and structure-preserving transformations. Ph.D. dissertation, MIT, Cambridge, MA.

Emonds, Joseph. 1976. *A Transformational Approach to English Syntax: Root, Structure-Preserving and Local Transformations*. New York: Academic Press.

Fowler, H. Ramsey. 1983. *The Little, Brown Handbook*. 2nd edn. Boston, MA: Little, Brown.

Greenberg, Joseph (ed.). 1966. *Universals of Language*. Cambridge, MA: MIT Press.

Grimshaw, Jane. 1990. *Argument Structure*. Cambridge, MA: MIT Press.

Grodzinsky, Yosef and Tanya Reinhart. 1993. The innateness of binding and coreference. *Linguistic Inquiry* 24: 69–101.

Jackendoff, Ray S. 1977. *X-Bar Syntax: A Study of Phrase Structure*. Cambridge, MA: MIT Press.

Katamba, Francis, 1993. *Morphology*. New York: St. Martin's Press.

Koopman, Hilda and Dominique Sportiche. 1991. The position of subjects. *Lingua* 85: 211–58.

Larson, Richard. 1988. On the double object construction. *Linguistic Inquiry* 19: 335–91.

Longobardi, Giuseppe. 1994. Reference and proper names: A theory of N-movement in syntax and logical form. *Linguistic Inquiry* 25: 609–665.

Perlmutter, D. 1978. Impersonal passives and the Unaccusative Hypothesis. *Proceedings of the Berkeley Linguistics Society* 4: 157–89.

Reinhart, Tanya. 1976. The syntactic domain of anaphora, Ph.D. dissertation. MIT, Cambridge, MA.

Reinhart, Tanya. 1981. Definite NP-anaphora and c-command domains. *Linguistic Inquiry* 12: 605–35.

Reinhart, Tanya. 1983. *Anaphora and Semantic Interpretation*. London: Croom Helm.

Ross, John R. 1967. Constraints on variables in syntax. Ph.D. dissertation, MIT, Cambridge, MA.

Ross, John R. 1969. Auxiliaries as main verbs. In W. Todd (ed.), *Studies in Philosophical Linguistics* (series 1). Evanston, IL: Great Expectations Press, 77–102.

Slobin, Dan I. 1979. *Psycholinguistics*. 2nd edn. Glenview, IL: Scott, Foresman.

Stageberg, Norman. 1981. *An Introductory English Grammar*. 4th edn. New York: Holt, Rinehart & Winston.

Travis, L. 1984. Parameters and effects of word order variation. Ph.D. dissertation, MIT, Cambridge, MA.

Vendler, Zeno. 1967. *Linguistics in Philosophy*. Ithaca, NY: Cornell University Press.

1

Doing Science with Language
Introductory Concepts

1.1 What is Scientific Inquiry?

What differentiates a scientific inquiry from any other sort of inquiry or theorizing? One core feature of scientific inquiry is what we might term a **testable hypothesis**, one that makes predictions that we can test. A "testable" hypothesis is one that can potentially be falsified by data. Should data not match the predicted outcomes of such a hypothesis, then we might (1) reject the hypothesis in favor of a different one that makes better, more accurate predictions; (2) revise the hypothesis if the revision is straightforward; or, if there is no alternative hypothesis or obvious revision, (3) maintain the hypothesis but note the problem for future inquiry. In terms of getting at the truth of how something works, there is no great answer-book in the sky. The only tools that we have to discover the nature of things are hypothesis formation and testing. These form the basis of everything that we know about anything in the universe from a scientific standpoint.

Often, when people talk casually and dismissively about "theories" (e.g. "Oh, that's just a theory!"), they seem to mean raw speculation or wild and unsupported guesses. This isn't what scientists mean by the term. Let's consider a (**scientific**) **theory** to be an overarching framework of thought that embodies a collection of hypotheses – in the best case, ones that are borne out by data and thus have some empirical support. We can think of a theory as having what we might term **empirical weight** in direct proportion to the number of facts/amount of data that the hypotheses within that theory are successful in predicting/explaining. Some theory A can be considered "competitive" with another theory B if it can be shown that A has similar empirical weight to B, though the two theories might not explain all of the

Syntactic Analysis: *The Basics*   Nicholas Sobin
© 2011 Nicholas Sobin

same phenomena. But such comparisons are tricky. It may be that some theory has what appears to be a lot of empirical weight, but just can't explain certain nagging facts. Another theory comes along that can neatly predict/explain these nagging facts, though it may otherwise be incomplete and in need of some "filling out." It has sometimes turned out that the theory which could explain the "nagging facts" was in the end the right one.

Here's a quick example of the latter case. How would you answer the question, "Did the sun rise this morning?" Nearly everyone would say "Yes." The basis for this answer lies not in how the universe actually works, but in the visual impression that we have, and possibly in the medieval (and earlier) belief (based on such visual impressions) that the earth was the center of the universe and everything in the sky was going around it. That earth-centered ("Ptolemaic") theory of the universe was based on a vast multitude of observable facts – the sun, the moon, and every star appeared simply to be going around the earth. Further, no one on the earth had (or has) any direct sensation of the earth moving (rotating). However, there are five objects (the five visible planets) that didn't simply pass by in a linear fashion, but instead appeared to backtrack in their courses (something called "retrograde" motion). For those objects, the earth-centered view had no good explanation. But, if we count each of the smoothly progressing star paths as a "fact," then given the thousands of visible stars, it looks like the earth-centered view predicts the large mass of facts correctly, with only five exceptions – not too shabby. But completely wrong! Copernicus's work (and that of others) to explain the five exceptions put the sun, not the earth, in the center of the "solar system" (a new concept) with only the moon circling the earth, and this view has ultimately proved correct. Further, the sun never rises – the earth rotates.

This little story has two major points. First, hypotheses/theories based purely on visual impressions (doing science by looking out the window) might be quite wrong – you need experimentation and theorizing. And second, a theory that can make sense of the nagging facts, even though it doesn't match sensory experience or immediate intuition, may turn out to be the right one. So doing scientific inquiry isn't always easy, but it is essential to understanding how things in the world actually work.

1.2   The Science of Language – Linguistics

Linguistics is the scientific study of human languages and the human language capacity. Our understanding of how human languages are structured and learned is only advanced by hypothesis formation and testing. Human language is a strongly subconscious mental faculty. While all humans are able to acquire at least one language at an early age and are able to speak it and understand it almost effortlessly, they have no conscious access to it. Often the "rules" that they firmly believe to hold in a language are wrong, even ridiculously off the mark, and are not followed by anyone speaking the language. Here's an example.

What is a pronoun? Many, maybe most, would say that it is a word that substitutes for a noun. Let's test that idea. Consider the noun *book* in (1):

(1) The red book is over there.

If you actually substitute a pronoun for the noun, you get (2), something that no English speaker would ever say:

(2) *The red it is over there.

What pronouns actually do is substitute for an abstract unit of structure called a *noun phrase*, a noun and all the words that immediately go with it. In (1), that would be *the red book*, and substituting *it* for *the red book* gives us the possible sentence (3):

(3) It is over there.

Looking at this in terms of hypothesis testing, what we have just done is to compare two hypotheses, one stating that pronouns substitute for nouns, and another stating that pronouns substitute for NPs, and tested them. The first makes two incorrect predictions, namely that (2) is good and that (3) is impossible. The second hypothesis makes two correct predictions, namely that (2) is impossible and that (3) is good. So, we think the second hypothesis is correct, at least insofar as we can tell from such testing. And therefore we also think that there is such a thing as an NP, even though we can't directly observe it.

An important perspective here is that such testing is the only means that we have to discover things. We can't ever prove that something is ultimately right. The most we can say is that as far as we can tell from advancing and testing testable hypotheses, some particular vision of how things are (a theory) is the best that we can come up with. Those are the limitations of scientific inquiry.

1.3 The Cognitive Revolution

Alongside the goal of understanding how human language grammars are structured is the goal of explaining how human language grammars are **acquired** by children. Linguists use the term **acquisition** to refer to **subconscious learning**, the sort of learning that is characteristic of human language grammar. Young children hear only a relatively small number of sentences (relative to the infinitely many available ones) from which they appear to "learn the language." No one tells them anything directly about the grammatical system underlying the language – in fact, linguists are still trying to discover what it consists of and how it works! Nonetheless, it is the grammatical system that a child must acquire in order to be able to speak the language, and, miraculously, that is exactly what each child manages to do. Though no one knows the details of how this is accomplished, there are some general ideas about how it works that are very likely on the right track. Here, we'll first consider a couple of what we might term "common sense" approaches to explaining language acquisition that don't actually pan out. Then we'll consider a more promising line of thought on the problem of acquisition.

1.3.1   Reinforcement

One early view of how language is acquired/learned is based on the stimulus–response model of learning. The idea is that positive and negative reinforcement would provide the "fundamental basis" for language "learning." I use the term "learning" here, since this would to some extent be the "conscious" learning of language. There are a number of problems with this view.

First, if the learner were to say a sentence like "Don't take some apples" and was told "No, that's wrong," the learner would not know what in particular was wrong, since the phrase "some apples" is perfectly correct in many circumstances. If the learner were told more specifically, "Don't say 'some'," then could that mean that the learner should never say it? Even if the learner were given a corrected form as in "Say 'Don't take *any* apples'," this still isn't sufficiently informative about why or when to say *any* (e.g. perhaps you're not supposed to say *some* with the word *apples*, or perhaps you're not supposed to say the word *some* after the word *take*, etc.). In sum, negative reinforcement and even corrections are much too ambiguous to drive language (grammar) learning/acquisition.

Second, studies show that when children are corrected, the corrections are mostly about the truth/accuracy of what the learner is saying and not about grammatical form. The amount of correction of sentence form that actually takes place is fairly minimal, far too minimal to be the basis for language learning/acquisition.

Third, studies show that children are not even capable of reproducing a "corrected" form before they are ready to do so, that is, before the grammar in their heads has developed to the point that that form is a possible production. Before this time, children famously persist in producing the **learner's forms** (utterance forms unique to children acquiring a language), regardless of the amount of correction that they are exposed to. It appears then that reinforcement is not and could not be the central device by which children acquire language.

1.3.2 Imitation

A somewhat popular "common sense" notion of how children acquire/learn a language is that they do it through imitation. This idea collapses rather quickly, however, on some of the same grounds as reinforcement does. The simple fact is that children at particular stages of language acquisition are not capable of imitating adult forms. Further, they persist in learner's forms (*I don't want some apples*) that are distinct from adult forms, and for which there is no model. Thus, imitation offers no explanation whatever of why learner's forms arise at all. It is also worth noting that imitation is nothing but the imitation of sentence forms; it is not at all clear how a learner would or could proceed from such imitation to acquiring the grammatical system, which is what the learner actually must acquire in order to be able to produce any of the infinitely many possible sentences in the language. So imitation also appears to fail as a plausible central device for language acquisition.

1.3.3 Innateness: Principles & Parameters

No one has been able to construct a plausible theory of how a child might use only the sentences that she or he hears to develop an explicit grammar of a language. The alternative is to think that perhaps human children are "hard-wired" to learn the language(s) in the surrounding environment. That is to say, the human brain may be genetically programmed for recognizing language input and knowing how to use it to construct the grammar for the language which that input exemplifies. Some general facts suggest that this is the correct approach.

First, all children go through the same general "stages" of language acquisition, regardless of which particular language is being acquired. These stages include a **One-Word Stage**, in which the child creates only single-word expressions (though the intended meaning is more complex); a **Two-Word Stage**, in which two and only two words may be put into a sentence, regardless of the complexity of the intended meaning; and then a **Tele-graphic Stage**, in which three or more content words (nouns, verbs, etc.) may be used to form longer sentences, but **function words** (e.g. *the, a, at, on, be,* etc.) are still largely absent. Children then proceed to develop use of the function words, along with developing more complex sentences. Though the stages and the reasons for them are not fully understood and are still the object of much research, the very presence of such cross-linguistically uniform stages strongly points to the presence of an innate program for language acquisition.

Second, children acquiring the grammar of a language produce normally irregular adult word forms (e.g. *swam*) as regular (e.g. *swimmed*), again without any external model for such regularization. This is one of many clear indications that children are subconsciously forming rules and using them broadly. Children learning English show this behavior in regularizing irregular verb forms (such as *swimmed*) and irregular noun forms (so that *feet* becomes *foots*, and plural *fish* becomes *fish(i)es*).

Although it is clear that children are acquiring the rules of a grammar, until recently it was not clear how they were going about it. When linguists attempt to discover grammatical rules, both **positive data** (data about which word sequences are 'good' sentences in the language) and **negative data** (data about "bad" word sequences, ones that are not sentences in the language) are crucial. That is, linguists have to know what the speaker both can and cannot do in forming sentences. For example, the subconscious grammar of English allows you to say, *Who saw what?* and *What did Mary see?* but not * *What did who see?*. (The * marks a sentence that is not possible in the language.) Such positive and negative data are crucial to discovering the rules that regulate the appearance of *wh* words like *what* and *who*. (In fact, such data are needed in any science – chemistry, for instance, is founded on information about which elemental combinations are possible and which are not.) If a child were discovering the rules of the grammar like a linguist (or any scientist) does, then the child would also need both positive and negative data. However, research in child language acquisition has shown that the *primary data* (all of the language input that a child hears and uses to subconsciously construct the grammar of the surrounding language) contains almost exclusively positive data. (Recall what was said above about correction.) Key negative data as exemplified above are simply absent from the primary data, and the few negative data that are present are of questionable value. This indicates that the child could not be working at grammar construction like a linguist does. So on what basis does a child construct her or his grammar? How does a child do it with only positive data, something that no scientist could do?

A recent and very promising theory of how children form the grammar of a language is what is called the **Principles & Parameters model**. The idea is that while much information key to forming a grammar comes from the primary data, the framework for constructing a grammar is inborn/"hard-wired" into human cognition in the form of **Principles** and **Parameters**. We can think of Principles as inviolable rules that must be followed in the construction of a grammar for any language. These are an inherent part of the innate human language capacity, something that has been given the label **Universal Grammar(UG)**. Every human is born with it, and it is essential to allowing each human being as a child to discover the grammar of the surrounding language. Parameters form another part of UG. They are also rules of grammar formation that must be followed, but they contain an "open setting" whose value is determined by relevant items in the primary data. This conception of the nature of language acquisition is in its infancy and needs a lot of filling out – there has been and continues to be a lot of debate about what the actual

Principles and Parameters are. However, given that children only have positive primary data to work from in constructing a grammar, it is still the most promising general theory of language and language acquisition that has been proposed thus far.

We will not try to exemplify particular Principles or Parameters at this immediate point, since we haven't established enough of a linguistic analysis to make this exercise very meaningful or contentful. However, as we proceed through our development of a linguistic theory, we will note and consider various possible candidates.

In the chapters to follow, we'll try to accomplish three things. First, we'll introduce terms and concepts basic to the study of human language, and especially syntax; second, we'll explore the operational details of particular hypotheses/theories of syntactic structure; and third, we'll put some emphasis on argumentation and hypothesis testing – the sort of work that linguists actually carry out in order to advance linguistic theory.

Summary Points of This Chapter

- A "theory" in the empirical sciences is an overarching view of how some part of the world works based on successfully tested hypotheses.
- Linguistic theory is a theory of how the grammatical systems that produce human languages are built and how they are acquired.
- Linguistics, like all empirical sciences, employs hypothesis testing to advance linguistic theory.
- Language acquisition, the subconscious learning of the grammatical system of a language, may to a large extent be "hard-wired," as indicated in part by the existence of cross-linguistically uniform stages of acquisition.
- Universal Grammar, the "hard-wired" basis for any language-particular grammar, may involve completely fixed Principles, and partially fixed Parameters, the latter allowing for some of the differences in sentence structure that different languages exhibit.

2

The Structure and Classification of Words

2.1 The Problem of Word Classification

Before discussing syntax, it is important to have some notion of what sorts of words exist. This is so because syntax is about the formation of sentences from words and, with a moment's reflection, you will quickly realize that when you're forming a sentence, the words can't just go anywhere – they seem to have to go in particular places relative to each other. The fact that word positioning is very limited indicates that there are **word classes**, groupings of words differentiated by sentence position.

When speakers "know" a language, a part of what they know is the vocabulary of that language. Let's refer to this mental dictionary as the **lexicon** of the language. Further, let's refer to the various word classes as **lexical categories**, since it is membership in one or another such category that dictates where a word can appear in a sentence. A problem that is preliminary to doing any syntactic analysis at all is that of discovering what the various lexical categories are, and which words belong in which category. Traditional grammars of English approach this problem in the discussion of what they usually term "parts of speech." In what follows, we'll have a look at the traditional view and why it fails. Then we'll go on to establishing more viable grounds for cataloging words into lexical categories.

Syntactic Analysis: *The Basics*   Nicholas Sobin
© 2011 Nicholas Sobin

2.2   The "Traditional" Approach

Traditional classroom grammars of English often group the words of English into the eight categories in (1):

(1)   **Typical "8" parts-of-speech list**
       Noun, pronoun, verb, adjective, adverb, preposition, conjunction, interjection.

How do we know which words of English belong in which category? *The Little, Brown Handbook*, like many traditional texts, offers the characterizations in (2) of some of the categories.

(2)   **Traditional definitions of parts of speech** (*The Little, Brown Handbook* (Fowler 1983))
       • **Nouns** name. . . .. Whatever exists or can be thought to exist has a name. Its name is a noun. (p. 128)
       • **Verbs** express an action, an occurrence, or a state of being. (p. 129)
       • Most **pronouns** substitute for nouns and function in sentences as nouns do. (p. 130)
       • **Adjectives** describe or modify nouns and pronouns. **Adverbs** describe the action of verbs, and also modify adjectives, other adverbs, and whole groups of words. (p. 136)
       • **Prepositions** are connecting words. (p. 139)
       • The word *and* is a coordinating **conjunction**. (p. 152)

These are commonly known definitions – what is the problem with simply using these? The problem is that this is an implausible and unusable system of classification. To see this, let's consider what a good system of classification should be like.

Three characteristics of any good classificatory system are listed in (3).

(3)   **Characteristics of a good taxonomy/classificatory system**
       a. exhaustiveness
       b. unambiguous criteria of classification
       c. single (set of) classifying principle(s)

An example of a good classificatory system is the Table of the Elements used in chemistry. First, it is exhaustive, meaning that all of the elements appear there. If a new element is discovered, it would simply be added to the table, as has often been done. Second, classification of one or another element is unambiguous – every element is classified according to its **atomic number,** a number indicating the number of protons in its nucleus, and no element can be in more than one category. Should we come across an element (say in a meteorite) whose identity we are uncertain of, by establishing its atomic structure, we should discover unambiguously that it either belongs to a known element class (e.g. despite appearances it is gold or iron, etc.) or that it is a "new" element that we would add to the general table – one with a different atomic number from all others. Third, all elements are classified by the same standard, making the various classes comparable and mutually exclusive. Thus the Table of the Elements classifies all elements in the same way, according to atomic structure.

Now, looking back at the parts-of-speech classification and the accompanying definitions, serious problems with this classificatory system become evident. First, the system is not exhaustive. There are various words that lack a category. For instance, the word *to* appearing in front of verbs in infinitive form (*to sing*) has no category. (To verify this, look *to* up in a dictionary that classifies words according to the traditional system, which most do.) The word *not* is sometimes called an adverb; however, it does not position itself in a sentence like any other adverb. This is illustrated in the sentences of (4), which compare the possible positioning of the adverb *quickly* to the possible positioning of *not*.

(4)   a. *Quickly* she closed the book. **Not* she closed the book.
      b. She *quickly* closed the book. **She *not* closed the book.
      c. She closed the book *quickly*. **She closed the book *not*.
      d. **She did *quickly* close the book. She did *not* close the book.

Words like *the* (Determiners) are sometimes called adjectives, but generally they do not interchange with adjectives. There are other examples, but the general point is that the parts-of-speech system is far from exhaustive.

Second, this system has ambiguous criteria for classification. For instance, it is stated above that you can identify something as a noun if it names something. The word *hungry* names something, namely a state of lacking food, but it's not a noun. It's an adjective. A baseline test of whether a criterion of classification is unambiguous is whether or not you could use it to classify words in a language that you don't speak (as linguistic anthropologists often must do). You would quickly discover that the criteria listed in (2) above are virtually useless. It would take something else to do the job.

Third, the criteria listed in (2) aren't consistent or unified. They do not involve a single principle or set of principles. The criteria for identifying nouns and verbs are "semantic" – they try to classify based on what the word means. The criterion for identifying pronouns is not semantic but "positional" – it tries to establish whether a word is a pronoun by where it goes (incorrectly claiming that a pronoun goes where a noun goes). The criterion for identifying adjectives is not semantic or positional but "functional" – it tries to identify adjectives in terms of what they do.

In terms of "good" classification, the traditional parts-of-speech system is a real mess. So how can we more adequately tackle the problem of word classification in a language?

2.3   Form and Position

Linguists generally turn the problem around and classify words based on where they go relative to each other in sentences, and in some cases how they are "shaped," that is, what prefixes, suffixes, etc. they might interact with or contain. In fact, this is probably how your brain solves the problem of learning and classifying words too. If you hear a new word in a sentence, that can tell you a lot. Consider the sentence in (5):

(5)   Mary blomed the apple.

What is *blomed*? Whatever it means, you can tell right away that it must be a verb because (i) it's going where a verb would go in the sentence, and (ii) it has the ending *-ed* meaning past tense, which only appears on verbs – whatever *blom* means, it happened in the past. So the problem is reduced to figuring out the meaning of what we now think is the verb *blom*. To develop this approach to classification further, let us introduce some necessary distinctions in the analysis of words.

2.4   Morphemes

As noted earlier, we refer to the mental dictionary as a lexicon. Each item listed in the lexicon of a language is a **lexical entry**. Are all of the lexical entries just words? It is probably not that simple. In sentence (5), the fact that you would recognize *blomed* as the past tense form of a verb indicates that you (using the grammar operating in your head) tear words apart into smaller meaningful bits. The fact that the ending *-ed* has a meaning on its own but is not a word indicates that your lexicon contains some meaningful elements that are smaller than a word. These are called **morphemes** – a morpheme is a minimal sequence of sounds with a meaning. By this definition, a single word like *books* contains two morphemes (two minimal meaningful parts), the **root** *book*, and the **suffix** *-s*, meaning **plural** (more than one). Roots are the core morphemes that a word is built on. Suffixes are endings that follow a root. Roots may be **free** or **bound**. A free root can appear as a word on its own (e.g. *book* or *walk*). A bound root cannot. Most English roots are free, but this is often not true of other languages. In Spanish, verb roots are bound – they always appear with an ending of some sort. For instance, the Spanish verb *jugar* '(to) play' in its various forms always minimally involves (a form of) the root *jug* and some suffix – the root can never be said by itself. The morphemes that attach to roots to form **complex words** (words of more than one morpheme) are called **affixes**. They include suffixes, **prefixes**, **infixes**, and **circumfixes**. Prefixes such as *un*-in the word *untangle* precede the root. Infixes actually intrude into the root – English has no examples of this, so we won't worry about them here. English used to have circumfixes, a simultaneous prefix–suffix combination, and modern German still does. For instance, one form of the German verb *machen* '(to) make' (root: *mach*; infinitive suffix: *-en*) is the word *gemacht* 'made' (past participle form), containing the root and the past participle circumfix *ge- -t*. Affixes are bound – they do not occur as words by themselves. Now if the lexicon is a list of roots and affixes, how do these get together to form complex (multi-morphemic) words? A partial answer may lie in considering affixes in more detail.

2.5   Affix Types

Two prominent types of affix exist in the lexicon: **inflectional affixes** and **derivational affixes**. Inflectional affixes simply give you all of the different forms that a word of a given lexical category can appear in. For example, a verb has five possible forms, as illustrated in (6). This range of possible verb forms is called the **verb paradigm**. *Jump* illustrates the forms of a "regular" verb, and *break* illustrates one way in which "irregular" verbs are formed.

(6)   **Verb paradigm**

Form name	Affix	"Regular" form	"Irregular" form
bare form	–	jump	break
present tense	$-s_{pres}$	jump**s**	break**s**
past tense	$-ed_{pst}$	jump**ed**	br**o**ke_
present participle	$-ing_{presprt}$	(is) jump**ing**	(is) break**ing**
past participle	$-ed/en_{pstprt}$	(has) jump**ed**	(has) br**oken**

There is also a **noun paradigm**, as illustrated in (7), and a **comparable paradigm**, as in (8).

(7)   **Noun paradigm**

Form name	Affix	"Regular" form	"Irregular" form
bare form	–	car	ox
plural	$-s_{pl}$	car**s**	ox**en**

(8)   Comparable paradigm

Form name	Affix	"Regular" form	"Irregular" form
bare form	–	smart	good
comparative	$-er_{cmpr}$	smart<u>er</u>	bett<u>er</u>
superlative	$-est_{sprl}$	smart<u>est</u>	be<u>st</u>

Since we're only dealing with morphology as needed for facilitating the study of syntax, we won't go into much more detail on variation in lexical forms. It is simply worth noting here that in irregular forms, roots and affixes may change form (e.g. *break/broke*), or even lose their phonetic form altogether (e.g. *good/better*).

Derivational affixes comprise another major class of affixes. Whereas inflectional affixes create the different possible forms of the same word (the inflectional paradigms), derivational affixes are used to create new, different words. English has robust derivation, as illustrated in (9) below. Partly for efficiency, we will use formulae like $[_N$V -ance]. This particular one should be read as follows: "the suffix *-ance* attaches to the right of a verb (V) and these two pieces form a noun (N)." The listing for a prefix such as $[_V$ re-V] should be read as "the prefix *re-* attaches to the left of a verb (V) and the two together create another verb (V)." Since affixes don't simply go onto roots but may also attach to complex (multi-morphemic) forms, let's use the term **stem** to refer to any simple or complex form that can take an affix. The list of derivational affixes in (9) contains some, but certainly not all, of the derivational affixes of English. Where examples do not appear, the affix has been listed in a preceding group.

(9)   **Derivational affixes**
      N-forming affixes:

$[_N$ V -al$_1$]	arriv<u>al</u>, approv<u>al</u>, recit<u>al</u>
$[_N$ V -ance]	appear<u>ance</u>, accept<u>ance</u>, reli<u>ance</u>
$[_N$ V -er]	bak<u>er</u>, cook<u>er</u>, toast<u>er</u>, sail<u>or</u>, advis<u>or</u>
$[_N$ V -ion]	act<u>ion</u>, relat<u>ion</u>, vacat<u>ion</u>, elect<u>ion</u>
$[_N$ Aj -ity]	rar<u>ity</u>, scarc<u>ity</u>, pur<u>ity</u>, drivabil<u>ity</u>, real<u>ity</u>
$[_N$ Aj -ness]	close<u>ness</u>, friendli<u>ness</u>, helpful<u>ness</u>, near<u>ness</u>
$[_N$ Aj -th]	tru<u>th</u>, streng<u>th</u>, wid<u>th</u>, dep<u>th</u>, leng<u>th</u>

      Affixes taking an N-stem:

$[_{Aj}$ N -ful]	wonder<u>ful</u>, aw<u>ful</u>, fear<u>ful</u>, force<u>ful</u>, beauti<u>ful</u>
$[_{Aj}$ N -ly$_1$]	friend<u>ly</u>, sister<u>ly</u>, world<u>ly</u>, woman<u>ly</u>
$[_{Aj}$ N -less]	friend<u>less</u>, power<u>less</u>, help<u>less</u>, error<u>less</u>
$[_{Aj}$ N -wide]	nation<u>wide</u>, city<u>wide</u>, country<u>wide</u>

V-forming affixes:

[v Aj -ize]	real<u>ize</u>, actual<u>ize</u>, national<u>ize</u>, visual<u>ize</u>
[v Aj -ify]	pur<u>ify</u>, fals<u>ify</u>, rect<u>ify</u>, clar<u>ify</u>
[v Aj -en]	redd<u>en</u>, soft<u>en</u>, whit<u>en</u>, black<u>en</u>
[v re-V]	<u>re</u>play, <u>re</u>do, <u>re</u>make, <u>re</u>write
[v un₁- V]	<u>un</u>do, <u>un</u>tie, <u>un</u>leash, <u>un</u>cage

Affixes taking a V-stem:

[Aj V -ive]	act<u>ive</u>, relat<u>ive</u>, submiss<u>ive</u>, divis<u>ive</u>
[v re-V]	
[v un₁- V]	
[N V -al₁]	
[N V -ance]	
[N V -er]	
[N V -ion]	
[Aj V -able]	wash<u>able</u>, driv<u>able</u>, work<u>able</u>, do<u>able</u>

Aj-forming affixes:

[Aj V -able]	
[Aj V -ive]	
[Aj N -ful]	
[Aj N -ly₁]	
[Aj N -wide]	
[Aj un₂- Aj]	<u>un</u>happy, <u>un</u>related, <u>un</u>true, <u>un</u>important
[Aj N -al₂]	nation<u>al</u>, relation<u>al</u>, accident<u>al</u>, pivot<u>al</u>

Affixes taking an Aj-stem:

[N Aj -ity]	
[N Aj -ness]	
[Aj un₂- Aj]	
[v Aj -ize]	
[v Aj -ify]	

Av-forming affixes:

[Av Aj -ly₂]	quick<u>ly</u>, quiet<u>ly</u>, unwitting<u>ly</u>, truthful<u>ly</u>
[Av N -wise]	time<u>wise</u>, temperature<u>wise</u>

One more thing to note is that among both inflectional and derivational affixes, there are **homonyms**, different morphemes that share the same phonetic form. Some examples are the plural affix -*s* going on nouns (*books*) and the present tense -*s* going on verbs (*likes*); the suffix -*ly* going on adjectives to form adverbs (*quickly*) and the suffix -*ly* going on nouns to form adjectives (*friendly*); and the prefix *un*- going on verbs meaning to 'undo' or 'free-up' (*untie*) and the prefix *un*- going on adjectives meaning 'not' (*unhappy*).

2.6 Affixes at Work: Word Formation

Now we face an interesting question: if the lexicon is a list of morphemes, then how are these morphemes combined to form complex words? Here, we need the notion **word formation rule**, a rule that combines a pair of morphemes into a single form. To develop a first approximation of this idea, let us consider further the concept of lexical entry. For a listing of a morpheme in the lexicon to be usable, what minimal information must it contain? First, it must tell us the **form** of the morpheme. (Here, we've simply been using spelled form, but it would actually have to contain information about pronunciation.) Second, it would have to indicate the **meaning** of the morpheme. And third, we would need information about its **lexical category**, since we have to know where it might go in a sentence or what other morphemes it might combine with. The lexical entries for root morphemes such as *pure*, *drink*, and *friend*, among others, are as in (10).

(10)   **Some sample lexical entries for root morphemes**
        Form and category: **Meaning:**
        [$_{Aj}$ pure]   'untainted'
        [$_{Aj}$ rare]   'not common'
        [$_V$ drink]   'consume liquid'
        [$_V$ jump]   (etc.)
        [$_V$ visit]
        [$_N$ friend]
        [$_N$ world]

That is, *pure* is an adjective meaning 'untainted', etc. Notice that the lexical category information on a root is simple – N, or V, or Aj, etc. But looking at the lexical entries for derivational affixes in (9), the category information is more complex. It tells us what lexical category the affix attaches to and the category of the lexical form that is created. So it's possible that word formation works something like this. Perhaps the category information that we see on derivational affixes is **dynamic** – that is, it is a command to create the structure that that listing for the derivational affix encodes. Thus, if we have the verb *drink* as in (11a) and the affix *-able* as in (11b), then we can follow the category information given for *-able* to produce *drinkable*, as in (11c):

(11)   a. [$_V$ drink]
        b. [$_{Aj}$ V -able]
        c. [$_{Aj}$ [$_V$ drink] -able]

Here, we've simply substituted the verb lexical entry in (11a) into the "V" slot of (11b) to get (11c). By doing such substitutions, we can create all sorts of complex words. Consider the word *unrepurifiable*. It would form as in (12):

(12)   a. $[_{Aj}$ pure$]$ + $[_V$ Aj -ify$]$ $\Rightarrow$ $[_V [_{Aj}$ pure$]$ -ify$]$

     b. $[_V [_{Aj}$ pure$]$ -ify$]$ + $[_V$ re-V$]$ $\Rightarrow$ $[_V$ re-$[_V [_{Aj}$ pure$]$ -ify$]]$

     c. $[_V$ re-$[_V [_{Aj}$ pure$]$ -ify$]]$ + $[_{Aj}$ V -able$]$ $\Rightarrow$

                                       $[_{Aj} [_V$ re-$[_V [_{Aj}$ pure$]$ -ify$]]$ -able$]$

     d. $[_{Aj} [_V$ re-$[_V [_{Aj}$ pure$]$ -ify$]]$ -able$]$ + $[_{Aj}$ un$_2$- Aj$]$ $\Rightarrow$

                                     $[_{Aj}$ un$_2$- $[_{Aj} [_V$ re-$[_V [_{Aj}$ pure$]$ -ify$]]$ -able$]]$

Such a system correctly predicts in many cases whether a given morpheme combination is possible or impossible. As just seen, it correctly predicts that *unrepurifiable* is a possible word. What about an impossible word like **purable*? The above rules would correctly disallow this possibility since the "rule" combining *-able* with something requires that that something be a verb, but *pure* is an adjective. So the combination is correctly excluded.

2.7   Adding Inflections

Finally, how are inflectional affixes added to stems to get words like the plural noun form *impurities*? All inflections seem to attach in the same way. They attach to a stem of a given lexical category and preserve that category – in fact, they are characteristic of it. So we might assume that inflectional affixes are listed in the lexicon perhaps as in (13):

(13)   **Lexical entries for inflectional affixes**

Form:	Meaning (first approximation):
$[_N$ N -s$_{pl}]$ or,	-'plural'
$[_V$ V -s$_{pres}]$	-'now'
$[_V$ V -ed$_{pst}]$	-'past'
$[_V$ V -ing$_{prsprt}]$	-'progressive'
$[_V$ V -ed/en$_{pstprt}]$	-'perfective'
$[_{Aj}$ Aj -er$_{cmpr}]$	-'more'
$[_{Aj}$ Aj -est$_{sprl}]$	-'most'

If the category information here is also dynamic, these affixes would yield forms as in (14):

(14)   a. $[_N [_N$ book$]$ -s$_{pl}]$
     b. $[_V [_V$ jump$]$ -ed$_{pst}]$
     c. $[_N [_N [_{Aj}$ im- $[_{Aj}$ pure$]]$ -ity$]$ -s$_{pl}]$

2.8   Inflectional Verb Affixes and Meaning

At first glance, one might assume that inflectional affixes have a simple meaning, as in (13) above. However, closer consideration of the meaning of these affixes reveals (i) that their meanings can be complex, and (ii) that their meanings may rely in part on other elements such as the verb they are attached to, and even other parts of the sentence. Further, the simple present tense verb affix -*s* has a complex meaning involving two types of information, information about the nominal subject and information about when and how things happen. We turn to considering these topics next.

2.8.1   Nominal meaning on verbs: agreement

First, the present tense -*s* reflects, or more accurately, "agrees with" certain features of the subject of the sentence. The subjects of sentences are typically NPs (Noun Phrases – recall the discussion in Chapter 1). Key features that characterize the nouns and pronouns which comprise subject NPs are given in the following chart (object forms such as *me*, *her*, *us*, and *them* would also bear these features):

(15)   **Features of nominal subjects**

Number:		singular	plural
Person:	first	I	we
	second	you	you
	third	she, he, it,	they, and
		and all singular nouns	all plural nouns

As an initial characterization, "Number" here refers to whether the nominal expression is singular ('one') or plural ('more than one'). "Person" can be thought of as a speech act feature as follows: first person is the speaker, second person is the hearer, and third person is anyone or anything else. These features are relevant to verbs because verb affixes in many languages reflect or "agree with" the subject on these features, something called **subject–verb agreement**. In English, the present tense verb suffix -*s* is used only when the subject is third person singular (e.g. *Mary sing -s*). Otherwise, only the bare verb form appears (e.g. *I sing*, or *The girls sing*). That is, the present tense -*s* "agrees" with the subject, and serves as an indication that the subject is third person singular nominal. Some languages have more such agreeing verb affixes. German verbs, for example, display the following singular agreement suffixes (along with other plural agreement suffixes not shown here):

(16)　**German verb suffixes (singular)**

Person:	first	-e	(*ich spiel -e* = 'I play')
	second	-st	(*du spiel -st* = 'you play')
	third	-t	(*sie spiel -t* = 'she plays')

Old English also had such a range of affixes, but all except for the third singular present, which is now *-s*, were lost in the evolution to Modern English. In sum, one of the meanings that *-s* conveys is that the subject is third person singular.

2.8.2　Temporal meaning

We normally refer to the *-s* and *-ed* verb affixes together as the **tense (or "temporal") affixes** because of the fact that they carry (in addition to information noted above about the subject of the sentence) **temporal meaning**, information about when and how things take place. In more detail, temporal meaning can be divided into two categories: **time reference** and **aspect**. "Time reference" ("when") has three possible values: **past**, **present**, and **future**. "Present" refers to the moment of speech ("now"). "Past" is a time earlier than that moment, and "future" is a time later than that moment. Thus, one element of the temporal meaning of *Mary walk -ed to the store* is that it took place earlier than "now," as indicated by the affix *-ed*. "Aspect" ("how") refers to the "nature" of an **action** or **state**. Some of the possible values for "aspect" are **single act/state**, **repeated act/state** ("frequentative/habitual"), **completed act** ("perfective"), and **continuing act** ("progressive"). **Perfective aspect** (meaning that an act has been completed) is usually indicated by using the perfective auxiliary verb *have* (e.g. *Mary has arrived*). **Continuative/progressive** aspect (meaning that the action is still underway), is often indicated by using the auxiliary progressive verb *be* (e.g. *Mary is jogging*). To go further, it is necessary to recognize a very basic distinction among verbs, one that interacts significantly with temporal meaning, the **stative/active** distinction. **Active verbs** are verbs which designate an action or activity such as *jump*, *write*, *sing*, and *put*. **Stative verbs** designate a state of being such as *know*, *want*, and *like*.

The system of assigning meaning to particular verb forms is very complex and beyond any brief explanation. Instead, let's consider some examples of verb forms to get an idea of the various factors involved.

First consider sentences such as those in (17):

(17)　a. Mary *know -s* the answer.
　　　b. Mary *sing -s*.

When the simple present affix -s is attached to a stative verb as in (17a), the speaker is asserting that the proposition that the sentence expresses is true "at the moment of speech" – Mary knows the answer "right now." However, when this -s is attached to an active verb, this isn't so – Mary isn't necessarily singing right now. Instead, it means something like 'Mary is in the habit of singing', or 'Mary sings frequently' ("present" time and "frequentative" aspect). To express the idea that the action is happening "now," active verbs require instead the **present progressive** verb form *be* V *-ing*, as in (18b), a form that stative verbs disallow or allow only rarely, as seen in (18a).

(18) a. *Mary *is (= be -s) know -ing* the answer.
    b. Mary *is (= be -s) sing -ing*.

As mentioned earlier, the verb form in (18b) also indicates that the action is "continuing" ("present" time and "progressive/continuative" aspect). It is worth noting here that in other languages such as Spanish and German, an active verb in simple present tense *does* mean that the action is taking place now, so the system of temporal interpretation for the English tense affixes is not universal.

Next, consider the fact that a sentence like (17b) may not mean 'present', but may instead mean 'future', a possible reading that comes across much more strongly in the context of a time adverb, as in (19):

(19) Mary *sing -s* at 5 p.m. (either 'present/habitual' or 'future/single act')

Note that an expression like *at 5 p.m.* is not itself biased toward past, present, or future (e.g. *I left at 5 p.m., It is now 5 p.m., I will leave at 5 p.m.*). So the adverb doesn't "push" the meaning toward future – that is just one of the possible meanings of the combination "active verb + -s" ("future" time and "single act" aspect). Stative verbs with present tense such as *know -s* in (17a) cannot have this "future" interpretation. Instead, you have to use additional verbs such as the modal verb *will* to express stative future, as in (20a). Further, stative verbs can be given "frequentative" aspect by adding adverbs such as *always*, as in (20b).

(20) a. Mary *will know* the answer.
    b. Mary *always know -s* the answer.

These additional expressions are not needed to get these interpretations with active verbs.

The simple past tense in many respects parallels the present tense in its relation to temporal meaning. Consider the sentences in (21):

(21)   a. Mary *want -ed* gloves.
       b. Mary *knew* (= *know -ed*) the answer.
       c. Mary *smoke -ed* a pipe.
       d. Mary *smoke -ed* a cigarette.

The stative verbs with past tense in (21a) and (21b) indicate a single state in the past. The simple past tense with an active verb as in (21c) may signal either a single act in the past or a past habit. The contrast in possible meanings between (21c) and (21d) reveals another factor that affects temporal interpretation – the object of the verb. Sentence (21c) has a much stronger past habitual reading than (21d) because a pipe is re-smokeable, but a cigarette is not. So (21d) tends strongly to mean only a single act in the past. However, if we substitute the plural form 'cigarettes" into (21d) giving *Mary smoke -ed cigarettes*, then the past habitual becomes a strong, overriding possibility.

As with present tense, there is even a sort of "future" time reference that past tense may express. Consider sentence (22):

(22)   Bill knew (= *know -ed*) that Mary left (*leave -ed*) at 5 p.m.

One of the possible meanings of (22) is that Bill knew that Mary was to leave at 5 p.m., a future single act relative to the past time expressed by *knew*. You have probably already noticed that the present progressive active verb forms such as *is* (= *be -s*) *sing -ing* in (16b) may also have a future single act interpretation, a reading again brought out more strongly in the presence of a time adverb, as in (23a). And, as (23b) shows, past progressive forms also have a parallel "future single act relative to a past time" reading, something like 'Mary was to sing at 5 p.m.'

(23)   a. Mary *is* (= *be -es*) *sing -ing* at 5 p.m.
       b. Mary *was* (= be -ed) *sing -ing* at 5 p.m.

2.8.3   Summary remarks on temporal meaning

It is apparent that there is no simple one-to-one relation between the verb affixes and temporal meaning. Rather, temporal meaning (time reference and aspect) is **compositional**; that is, it is somehow calculated on a combination of factors appearing in the sentence including (i) the tense affixes *-s* or *-ed*, (ii) the stative or active character of the verb, (iii) the possible presence of the aspectual verbs *have* and *be*, (iv) the possible presence of modal verbs like *will*, and (v) the features of other elements of the sentence such as whether an object is singular or plural, and whether it is reusable. This is just an initial characterization. A more in-depth analysis is beyond the scope of this work.

2.9 Final Remarks

Thus far, we have only scratched the surface of morphological analysis. It is far richer than what we have seen so far. The approach that we have developed is **generative**: rather than listing whole words in the lexicon, we have claimed that they are actually generated from morphemes by a system of rules. This is the approach that we will also take in dealing with syntax. There, it appears logically necessary to do so, since there are infinitely many possible sentences.

Summary Points of This Chapter

- The traditional system of word classification is inadequate for the purpose of linguistic analysis.
- Useful criteria for classifying lexical items include **morphological form** (how the item participates in inflection and derivation) and **position** (where the item can appear in sentences).
- The **lexicon** is a list of **morphemes** rather than words per se. **Complex words** are formed by **word formation rules**.
- The **tense affixes** are -*s* and -*ed*. Unlike -*ing*, whose presence on a verb is dictated by a preceding auxiliary verb *be*, the presence of the tense affixes is not dictated by any other verb. In this sense, they are "freely selected," much like the aspectual verbs (*have* and *be*) and the modal verbs (*can, could, will, would, may*, etc.) to express the temporal meaning of a given sentence.
- The **aspectual affixes** are the present participle affix -*ing* and the past participle affix -*en/ed*. Their presence is commonly dictated by the presence of the aspectual verbs *be* and *have*, respectively (e.g. *Mary is swimming*, and *Mary has chosen a hammer*).
- The tense affix -*s* on verbs expresses subject-related information (subject–verb agreement).
- The tense affixes and other elements do not have simple temporal meanings, but are a part of a system of determining temporal meaning based on a variety of factors. Temporal meaning is **compositional**.

Supplementary Notes and Problems

Notes on identifying members of the major lexical categories

To identify the members of major lexical classes, you often have to "manipulate" the words you are trying to classify (and even their surroundings), but

not to the extent of changing them into something else. It takes a little
to develop a sense for doing this.

Noun

form   often takes (a form of) the noun **inflectional** suffi
            sometimes takes certain **derivational** affixes to fo...
               words, e.g., /-ful$_{Aj}$/, or /-ly$_{Aj}$/
            sometimes identifiable by a "final" **derivational** suffix,
               e.g., /-ion/, /-er$_N$/, /-ity/, or /-th/

position fills the role of subject/object (an "argument" position)
               in a sentence
             may be accompanied by various articles (*a*, *the*, *some*,
               etc.)

Verb

form   takes many or all of the verb **inflectional** suffixes,
               e.g., /-s$_{pres-3rd-sg}$/, /-ed$_{pst}$/, /-ing$_{presprt}$/, or/-ed/en$_{pstprt}$/
            sometimes takes certain **derivational** affixes to form other
               words, e.g., /-able$_{Aj}$/, /-ion$_N$/, or /-er$_N$/
            sometimes identifiable by a "final" **derivational** suffix,
               e.g., /-ify/, or /-ize/

position fills the "verb" slot in a sentence (a "non-argument"
               position, i.e., not subject or object); that is, it could only
               be replaced by some other word analyzable as a verb
             may be accompanied by various "auxiliary" verbs

Adjective-

form   sometimes takes the "comparable" **inflectional**
               suffixes /-er$_{cmpr}$/ and /-est/
            sometimes takes certain **derivational** affixes to form other
               words, e.g., /-ly$_{Av}$/ or /-th/
            sometimes identifiable by a "final" **derivational** suffix,
               e.g., /-ive/, /-able/, or /-ful/

position may precede a noun or appear between an article
               and a noun
             may follow the verb *be* in a construction like
               Mary is __ (but so may a noun; therefore, you might have
               to appeal to other tests)
             sometimes positions with intensifiers such as *very, quite*,
               or *somewhat*

(Refer to Appendix 1 for similar criteria for identifying members of the minor
lexical categories.)

Problems

1. Use the affixation and positioning criteria to identify the class of each underlined word in the following passages.
    Sample answer: *Hiding* (in (a) below) is a verb because (i) it shows the verb suffix *-ing*, (ii), it could take other verb suffixes, (e.g. *hide -s*), (iii) it could take derivational affixes that go on verbs (e.g. *hideable, unhide-able*), (iv) it follows an auxiliary verb (*was*), and (v) it is positioned where another verb could substitute for it.

    a. Mary was <u>hiding</u> several <u>snakes</u> in her <u>strongest</u> cardboard box. Her <u>intentional</u> <u>deception</u> <u>caused</u> Bill <u>problems</u>. He <u>had</u> to <u>tell</u> the <u>manager</u> that the <u>strange</u> hissing <u>noises</u> were <u>caused</u> by a <u>leaky</u> <u>radiator</u>.
    b. <u>Mary</u> <u>takes</u> <u>long</u> <u>vacations</u> every <u>summer</u>. She <u>likes</u> to <u>go</u> to the <u>beach</u>, but the <u>sand</u> and <u>salt air</u> are pretty <u>rough</u> on her <u>fancy</u> <u>car</u>, so she <u>rides</u> on the <u>bus</u>.

2. Using the word formation rules discussed above for derivational and inflectional affixes, diagram the morphological structure of each of the following words.
    Sample answer: "friendliness" would be analyzed as
    [N [Aj [N friend] -ly] -ness].

    a. words (N)
    b. working (V)
    c. unclarity (N)
    d. repurified (V)
    e. carefully (Av)
    f. unhelpfulness (N)
    g. renationalized (V)
    h. unretiable (Aj)
    i. reuntiable (Aj)

3. Based on what has been said about temporal interpretation, and using your own intuitions, what is (/are) the possible temporal meaning(s) (time reference and aspect) of each of the following sentences?

    a. Mary has been painting.
    b. Max rides a bicycle at 7 a.m.
    c. Zelda was leaving on Saturday.
    d. Mary walked Fido on Sunday evening.
    e. Mary walked Fido on Sunday evenings.

4. (**Advanced**) It is possible to discover morphemes in another language by inspecting text in that language along with its translation and observing how the meaning changes as the text changes. Below are some data from Quechua, a native American language spoken in Peru and Bolivia. Quechua has verb suffixes that encode subject information. By inspecting the forms in (a) and their meanings, try to ascertain what the roots and affixes are that form Quechua verbs. Next, inspect the sentences in (b) and then (c). Try to extend your analysis of the Quechua lexicon to include other morpheme types, including additional verbs, nouns, and noun affixes. Finally, try to map out what the parts of a sentence are and how they line up to form a sentence.

Sample answer: By comparing the first two verb forms, we might hypothesize the following: *muna* is a verb root meaning 'want', *-ŋ* is a verb suffix meaning third person singular subject, and *-ni* is a verb suffix meaning first person singular subject.

a. **Verb forms**

munaŋ	'(s)he wants'
munani	'I want'
hap?iŋ	'he catches'
hap?ini	'I catch'

b. **Sentences (I)**

waɫpata munaŋ	'(s)he wants the chicken'
pʰuɫuta munaŋ	'(s)he wants the blanket'
waɫpata munaŋki	'you want the chicken'
uk pʰuɫuta munaŋki	'you want a blanket'
waɫpata hap?iŋ	'(s)he catches the chicken'
waɫpata hap?isaŋ	'(s)he is catching the chicken'
uk čilwita hap?isani	'I am catching a (little) chick'

c. **Sentences (II)**

waɫpa pʰawaŋ	'the chicken flies'
hwanito punuŋ	'Juanito sleeps'
alqu puriŋ	'the dog walks'
nikolasa pičaŋ	'Nicolasa sweeps'
nikolasa hwanitota rikʰusaŋ	'Nicolasa is seeing Juanito'
waɫpa alquta rikʰusaŋ	'the chicken is seeing the dog'

3

Determining the Structure of Sentences

Next we will tackle the question of how sentences are formed. As a preliminary, we should consider some basic facts about the sentences of a natural (human) language such as English. First, as was argued in the previous chapter, the words appearing in sentences seem to fall into particular "slots" – they can't simply be randomly re-ordered. That's one of the reasons for thinking that there are discrete lexical categories, each with its proper position(s) in a sentence. Words fall into restricted linear orders. Second, the number of possible sentences isn't just large; it is infinite. This is demonstrable as follows. There is no "longest" sentence in any human language; any given sentence can be made longer. Since there is no "longest" sentence, there must be infinitely many of them. Another indication of the infinite mass of sentences available is this: if you were given a particular sentence like *Jane has admired my aunt's picture* and asked to go to the library and look through every publication until you found it, you likely never would. There are far too many sentences, and even simple ones might be brand new. **Noam Chomsky** has given the name **linguistic creativity** to this human capacity to deal in new or "novel" utterances. Third, it appears that the words of a sentence do not go directly into the sentence per se, but instead are organized into **phrases**, sub-groups of words that in turn are used to form the structure of a sentence. There is considerable evidence that this is true, and we turn to this topic next.

Syntactic Analysis: *The Basics*   Nicholas Sobin
© 2011 Nicholas Sobin

3.1   Evidence for Phrase Structure

In Chapter 1, we saw evidence as in (1−3) below that pronouns don't substitute for nouns but rather for a unit of structure headed by a noun called a noun phrase (NP).

(1)   The red book is over there.

(2)   *The red it is over there.

(3)   It is over there.

As we will see, manipulating the form of sentences rarely involves words per se − it is **phrases** (also called **constituents**) that are the object of manipulation, and as we shall see, sentences are rich with phrasal structure. A phrase is a sequence of one or more words built around a **head** lexical item and working as a unit within a sentence. How can we discover which sequences (strings) of words in a sentence form phrases/constituents? A word sequence is shown to be a phrase/constituent if it exhibits one or more of the behaviors to be discussed below (that is, if it can be manipulated in one or more of the following ways). Establishing the phrasal structure of sentences using such tests is key to initially determining what the rules are that form sentence structure. That is, we have to establish something about what the structures of given sentences are before we can say anything about how those structures may be formed.

3.1.1   The movement test

A phrase and **only** a phrase can move. Therefore, movement is a test for phrasehood. Consider an "active" sentence like (4).

(4)   [The head librarian] put [an important book about syntax] on the desk.

When sentence (4) is made "passive" as in (5), the bracketed noun phrase (NP) sequences move.

(5)   [An important book about syntax] was put ___ on the desk by [the head librarian].

Single words from (4) cannot undergo such movement, as seen in (6).

(6)   *Book was put an important ___ about syntax on the desk.

Movement often leaves a tell-tale "hole" in the structure, indicated by the ___ in (5). Here, although *put* in active sentences must have a following NP (e.g. *Mary put [the book] on the desk*, and not **Mary put on the desk*), the ___ in (5) sounds fine and cannot be filled with another expression (e.g. **The book was put the pen on the desk*). Hence, the movement in (5) indeed leaves a tell-tale "hole" in the sentence.

It isn't only NPs that move. Verb phrases (VPs) may also move, as illustrated in (7):

(7) They said that Mary might write a book, and ...) [write a book] she will ___.

The bracketed VP in (7) moved from its normal end-of-sentence position to the front and again, a single word such as the verb can't do this (e.g. **... and write she did ___ a book*).

Adjective phrases (AjP) display the same movement, as seen in (8):

(8) (They said she is very smart, and ...) [very smart] she is ___.

Prepositional phrases (PP) can also be moved, as in (9):

(9) [On the lower shelf], Mary put the spaghetti ___.

Notice here too that you can't normally say **Mary put the spaghetti*, so again we see a hole created by movement.

3.1.2 The sentence fragment test

Only a phrase can form a viable sentence (S) fragment. Consider the various fragment responses in (10):

(10) a. What will Mary want?   [An expensive book]   (NP)
      b. What will Bill do   [Go to the races]/   (VP)
         tomorrow?   [Give a talk]
      c. How smart is Mary?   [Very smart]   (AjP)
      d. Where's Mary?   [At MIT]   (PP)

All of the bracketed responses are phrases, and only phrases can be used in this way.

3.1.3 The coordination test

Ordinary coordination offers robust evidence of phrasehood. Coordination differs from the other tests here in that single words may also coordinate.

But rather than being problematic, this use of coordination is instructive. Consider the "good" single-word coordinations in (11) and the "bad" ones in (12):

(11) a. day and night   (N and N)
      b. mowed and watered   (V and V)
      c. rare and expensive   (Aj and Aj)
      d. on and under.   (P and P)

(12) a. *day and under   (N and P)
      b. *mowed and night   (V and N)
      c. *on and rare   (P and Aj)

It is quite easy to think of sentences in which the lexical coordinations in (11) might occur, but not so for those in (12). What sets the good ones off from the bad ones? As a first approximation, we might formulate the "restriction" on coordination in (13):

(13) **The coordination restriction**
      Only identical types of elements may coordinate.

Now, consider the good coordinations in (14) and the bad ones in (15):

(14) a. [A boy] and [a girl]   (NP)
      b. [mowed the lawn] and [watered the flowers]   (VP)
      c. [very smart] and [quite clever]   (AjP)
      d. [over the river] and [through the woods]   (PP)

(15) a. *[a boy] and [over the river]
      b. * [watered the flowers] and [very smart]

If the same restriction is at work (and it is good science to assume that it is – all such rules should be as general as possible), then this indicates that phrases must exist, since in (14) and (15), they would be the "elements" referred to in restriction (13). So coordination provides interesting evidence for the existence of phrases.

3.1.4 The proform test

Thus far, we have referred to words like *she* and *they* as "pronouns," but as we've seen, these words don't correspond to nouns but instead to NPs. They might better be termed ProNPs. Other types of phrases also have such words that "target" (replace or refer to) them. These are illustrated in (16):

(16) a. ProNP (e.g. *he*): [The boy] left early ⇒ [He] left early
                                (not *The he left early*)
     b. ProVP (*do so*): Mary will [eat a hamburger], and Max will do so too.
                                (not *... and Max will do so a cheeseburger*)
     c. ProAjP (*so*): Mary is [very clever], and so is Bill.
     d. ProPP (*then/there*): Mary reads [in the morning], and Bill reads then too.
                                Mary went [to Berlin], and Max went there too.

Generally, a proform must always "target" (replace or refer to) a phrase.

3.1.5 The omissibility test

Some expressions in a sentence are optional, that is, omissible – they can be left out without affecting the basic meaning of the remaining sentence. These omissible expressions are always phrases, and so omissibility is a test of phrasehood. PPs and AjPs are commonly omissible, as in (17). ( )s within the sample sentences indicate the optional/omissible portion.

(17) a. Mary arrived ([in the afternoon]). – PP
     b. Mary is very clever, and Jane is ([very clever]) too. – AjP

In sum, what we now have is a variety of tests indicating the phrasehood of particular word sequences that may be present within a sentence. As may be apparent, certain phrases may be contained within other phrases, so sentence structures are **hierarchic**. We turn next to considering the structure of sentences.

3.2 Hierarchic Sentence Structure

If we were to apply the various tests of phrasehood to a sentence like the one in (18), the outcomes might be summarized in a structure like (19).

(18) A very expensive car was in the garage.

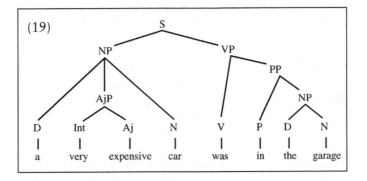

(Here, D = determiner ("article" in traditional terminology), Int = intensifier, and P = preposition.) Briefly, the sequence *very expensive* can be omitted or coordinated with ... *and quite attractive*; the sequence *a very expensive car* can be substituted for with the ProNP *it* or coordinated with ... *and a motorcycle*; the sequence *the garage* can be coordinated with ... *or the parking lot* or (due to its status as a location) may be replaced with *there*, yielding *in there*; the sequence *in the garage* may also be replaced by *there*, or coordinated with ... *or on the street*; finally the sequence *was in the garage* can be coordinated with ... *and got stolen*. You can also reverse (move) the NP under S and the PP under VP to get (20):

(20)   In the garage was a very expensive car.

All of these results point toward the structure in (19).

We might think of (19) as telling us all of the following information: the sequence *very expensive* forms an AjP. This AjP combines with the words *a* and *car* to form an NP. The words *the* and *garage* form another NP, and this NP combines with the preposition to form a PP. The verb and this PP together form a VP, and this VP combines with the NP headed by *car* to form the sentence (S). The diagram in (19) is called a **tree marker**, or simply a **tree** – the structure assigned to a sentence. What follows are some terms that are important for talking about trees:

(21)   **Some useful tree terms:**
   node/constituent/category: any formal "piece" of sentence structure (e.g. NP, VP, V, P, etc.)
   phrasal category: a syntactic category that contains one or more other categories (e.g. NP, VP, etc.)
   lexical category: a syntactic category that immediately dominates a lexical item (e.g. N, V, D, Aj, etc.)
   branch: a line in a tree marker connecting two nodes

tree (**marker**): an arrangement of nodes and branches assigned to a sentence by the rules of syntax

dominates: a category X **dominates** another category Y if there is a downward path of branches from X to Y, and X is the higher category

immediately dominates: a category X **immediately dominates** another category Y if there is a single branch connecting X and Y, and X is the higher category

mother: X is the **mother** of Y if X immediately dominates Y

daughter: Y is a **daughter** of X if X immediately dominates Y

sister: X is a **sister** of Y if X and Y share the same mother

We will make a lot of use of these and other terms as we proceed to develop our ideas about syntactic structure and the rules that create it.

Summary Points of This Chapter

- The sentences of human languages exhibit the following three basic properties: **linear** (left-right) **order, infinity** (an unbounded number of well-formed sentences, that is, ones that follow the rules of sentence formation), and **hierarchic organization** (internal phrasal structure).
- Hierarchic organization is evidenced in how sentences can be manipulated, the "**tests of phrasehood.**"
- These tests include **movement**, the ability to serve as a **sentence fragment**, the ability to **coordinate**, the ability to be the target of a **proform**, and **omissibility**.
- Such tests allow us to establish the hierarchic structure of sentences, something that must be known before we can begin to discover the rules responsible for such structure.

Problems

1. For each underlined sequence in the following sentences, use two different tests of phrasehood to argue that it is a phrase.
   a. The cat walked into the building.
   b. Mary is painting her room.
   c. The people who were carrying large signs seemed very agitated.

2. Use tests of phrasehood to determine the phrasal structure of the following sentences:
   a. The thieves have stolen a photo of a famous building.
   b. Mary might put the very expensive china on the highest shelf.

3. Sometimes evidence of phrasehood appears directly in naturally occurring sentences. Using elements found within each of the following sentences, say which test is in evidence and which word sequence is shown to be a phrase.
   a. Mary and the girl in the purple hat went to the movies.
   b. A person carrying a club and one holding a sign entered the building.
   c. The gymnast leapt onto the high beam, and she did so with almost no effort.
   d. Into the soup, Mary put a pair of old socks.
   e. A: What do you want to do? B: Go to the movies.

4. (**Advanced**) Here are some manipulations of a sentence of German. What phrases are evidenced in these manipulations?

   a. Der Junge hat den Hut auf den Boden gelegt.
      the boy   has the hat on the floor laid
      "The boy put my hat on the floor"
   b. Auf den boden hat der Junge den Hut gelegt.
   c. Den Hut hat der Junge auf den Boden gelegt.

5. (**Advanced**) **Logically valid** arguments are "airtight"—ones whose conclusion cannot be false if the premises leading to the conclusion are true. Here is an example, where P means 'premise', and C means "conclusion":

   P1: All dogs have a tail.
   P2: Max is a dog.
   C: Max has a tail.

   C logically cannot be false if P1 and P2 are true.

   We can frame tests of phrasehood as logically valid arguments as in the following example:

   P1: Only phrases move.
   P2: The word sequence *on the shelf* in the sentence *Mary put the expensive china on the shelf* can move, as in the following example: *On the shelf, Mary put the expensive china.*
   C: *On the shelf* is a phrase.

   It is important to note that the word *only* in P1 is crucial to the logical validity of the argument. If non-phrases can also move, then this argument does not go through—*on the shelf* could move and not be a phrase.
   P1s for the other tests of phrasehood are the following:

Only phrases may be substituted for by a proform;
Only phrases may be omitted;
Only phrases may be sentence fragments;
Only phrases (or single words) may be coordinated with *and* or *or*.

Select five word sequences from any of the sentences in problem 3 above, and for each word sequence, form a logically valid argument for its status as a phrase.

4

Rules of Sentence Structure
A First Approximation

Now that we've established that sentences have a structure, the next logical question is "Why?" How do sentences get a structure? This is a particularly formidable problem when one realizes how many sentences there are in any human language – infinitely many, as discussed earlier. This is easy to demonstrate. Take a sentence like *Mary likes bagels*. It can be extended into *Bill believes that Mary likes bagels*, which may in turn be extended into *Zoe thinks that Bill believes that Mary likes bagels*. What is the longest possible such extension? There is none – ideally, any such sentence could be extended further. Thus there is no "longest" sentence of English (or of any other language), and consequently the set of possible sentences (in any language) must be infinite.

Actually, this fact (that languages are infinitely large) points us toward a solution. Since no one could ever learn the sentences per se (there are too many), we must have some means of calculating or computing them. Most linguists believe that this is carried out by a "grammar," or computing system that each speaker possesses. The term **linguistic competence** was Chomsky's original term for this subconscious system of knowledge of language. And it is this computing system, now referred to as the **computing system for human language (C$_{HL}$)** that is at the heart of research in theoretical syntax. The big questions are (i) what are the contents of such a system (its elements and rules)? and (ii) how does a human child acquire such a system? Is it learned simply from exposure to language, or are aspects of it **hard-wired,** that is, innate in human cognition? As discussed earlier in Chapter 1, the latter possibility is referred to as the **innateness hypothesis.** Since we can't directly inspect any human language grammar (it's somehow embedded in everyone's brain), we might approach the problem of discovering the contents of such a grammar by studying something that is observable: the sentences that such a system can

Syntactic Analysis: *The Basics* Nicholas Sobin
© 2011 Nicholas Sobin

produce. Any human language grammar allows certain word sequences to form into sentences but disallows others from doing so. For instance, any speaker of English recognizes that (1a) is a good **acceptable** sentence of English (one that sounds "natural" to a native speaker), whereas (1b) is **unacceptable** – a word sequence that any speaker would recognize as impossible (noted with a "*"):

(1)   a. The cow jumped over the moon.
     b. *moon cow the the over jumped.

We might try to use the grammar's output of acceptable sentences along with consideration of what is unacceptable as the basis for trying to make inferences about what the system that produces such sentences is like. To the extent that we can construct a system that mimics (successfully predicts) the possible output of the real system, then we have reason to think that our constructed system is a successful model/theory of the real system.

The idea of acceptability as just presented is a little over-simple. Consider Chomsky's notorious sentence *Colorless green ideas sleep furiously*, which is semantic nonsense, but which has an **acceptable syntactic arrangement** that any speaker would recognize, in contrast to another sequence such as *furiously sleep ideas green colorless*, which is not only nonsense, but also unacceptable in its syntax. So when we speak of acceptability, we may use it on a number of levels.

4.1   Phrase Structure Grammar

One system which has enjoyed some success in modeling human language grammar is called **phrase structure (PS) grammar**. As its name suggests, it does not seek to describe whole sentences at once, but instead spells out the immediate contents of phrases, as detectable through tests of constituency. Since phrases can build on other phrases, ultimately we get sentences. The grammar in (2) is a good place to start:

(2)   **A simple PS grammar for English**

Unconflated rule form:
  1 S → NP VP
  2 S → NP Aux VP
  3 VP → V
  4 VP → V NP

  5 VP → V PP

  6 VP → V AjP

Conflated rule form:

rules 1–2:   S → NP (Aux) VP

rules 3–9: $VP \rightarrow V\ (NP) \left(\left\{ \begin{array}{l} NP \\ PP \\ AjP \end{array} \right\} \right)$

  7 VP → V NP NP   (These basic VP rules reflect the
  8 VP → V NP PP   various transitivity possibilities.)
  9 VP → V NP AjP
 10 PP → P NP   rule 10:   PP → P NP
 11 NP → N
 12 NP → D N
 13 NP → AjP N
 14 NP → D AjP N   rules 11–14:   NP → (D) (AjP) N
 15 AjP → Aj
 16 AjP → Int Aj   rules 15–16:   AjP → (Int) Aj

These rules are presented in two forms, an unconflated form spelling
out as a separate rule each phrasal possibility, and a conflated form,
which combines different but related phrasal possibilities into a single
rule. Thus the 16 unconflated rules can be reduced to 5 conflated rules.
We'll discuss the unconflated rules first, and then turn to their conflated
form.

4.1.1   PS rule basics

In these rules the " → " may be read as "consists of" or "contains." So rule 12,
for example, says that a N(oun) P(hrase) consists of first a D(eterminer) and
next a N(oun). This can be diagrammed as the tree in (3), assuming that D is
the, and N is *garage*.

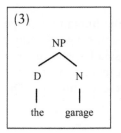

Rule 10 says that a P(repositional) P(hrase) consists
of a P(reposition) and an NP. If the P is *in*, and if the NP
is the one in (3), then rule (10) gives us the tree in (4).

Each of these PS rules simply states the mother–
daughter–sister relations among the relevant constituents. As you can probably guess at this point, applying
the needed rules would finally result in complete sentences, such as (18/19) from Chapter 3, as follows.

Rule 5 would allow us to combine the tree in (4) with
the verb *was*, as in (5).

Now we need to start constructing the subject NP.
Rule 16 allows us to combine the words *very expensive*
into an AjP, as in (6).

Next, rule 14 lets us combine the tree (6) with the
words *a* (= D) and *car* (= N) to create the subject NP, as
in (7).

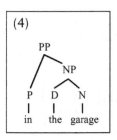

Finally, rule 1 allows us to combine the NP in (7) and
the VP in (5) into a S(entence), as in (8).

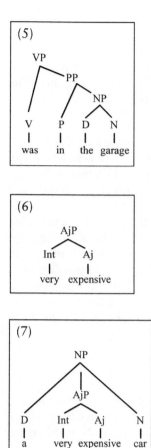

(5)

(6)

(7)

Recall that the sentence in (8) is one that we used earlier in Chapter 3 when we considered the tests of phrasehood. It has the structure that tests on the various word sequences pointed toward. Interestingly, the PS rules in (2) are able to replicate this structure. That is, these rules not only tell us that the word order is a possible sentence of English, but they also assign to that word order the "right" structure, the one that independent tests indicated earlier was present. Thus, we have a working model of a grammar for English that seems to be succeeding in modeling both how the words can line up and what their hierarchic arrangement is. As an initial hypothesis, this grammar looks pretty good. If we say that any "good" sentence must have an "S" at the top of its tree, must include under that S all of the words of the sentence, and may only use the PS rules as specified in (2) to build the tree, then these rules predict that the word sequence in (8) not only can but must have this structure – there is no other way that the PS rules can structure this sentence. Since this structure appears to be the right one, that is a good result indeed!

What of unacceptable word sequences? Let's make the following assumption. A sentence that is acceptable is also **grammatical** – it is producible by the rules of the grammar. For simplicity's sake, I will equate unacceptability (unnatural-sounding) with **ungrammaticality**: an **ungrammatical** word sequence will be one that the rules of the system cannot produce a complete tree for, where such tree production is the only means by which a sentence is produced. Here's what we mean. Consider an unacceptable/ungrammatical word sequence such as (9):

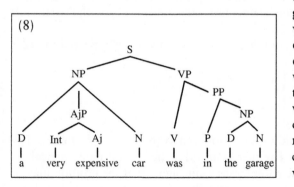

(8)

(9) *The was car garage the in

If the grammar could "tree" this sequence to S, then the grammar would (incorrectly) predict that (9) is a possible sentence. However, it cannot. The best we can do in trying to use the rules as written to analyze (assign a structure to) (9) is seen in (10).

(10)

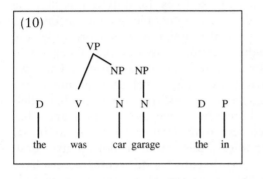

Since we are unable to analyze (9/10) as a sentence (S), this system, grammar (2), successfully predicts that the word sequence (9) is not a sentence of English. It is by proceeding along these lines, testing the grammar against other both possible and impossible sentences, that we can discover where the grammar hypothesized in (2) is successful, where it fails, and perhaps what we might do to address the failures.

4.1.2   The conflated form of the rules

The conflated rules in (2) impart all of the same structural information that the unconflated rules do. For instance, the conflated NP rule, repeated here as (11), says that when you construct an NP, there will always be an N at the right.

(11)   NP → (D) (AjP) N

The "()"s surrounding D and AjP here indicate that a D may or may not be present, and an AjP may or may not be present, but if either occurs, it is positioned relative to the other elements as indicated in (11), with D to the left edge and AjP to the left of N.

The VP rule is the most complex of the rules here. It is repeated in (12):

$$(12) \quad VP \rightarrow V(NP) \left(\left\{ \begin{array}{c} NP \\ PP \\ AjP \end{array} \right\} \right)$$

It states that in a VP, the V is always leftmost. It may (or may not) be followed by one or two other elements. The first is an NP. The second parenthetical set appears in curly braces. The parentheses again signal that the position may or may not be filled, and the curly braces signal that if you do select something here, it may be any one of the items in the vertical stack. Thus, this rule allows all of the same possibilities that are encoded in the whole set of unconflated VP rules.

What advantage is there to the conflated rules? As many have noted, the conflated rules are better at capturing significant generalizations about the structure of language, and of course, discovering such generalizations is a main aim of scientific research. For example, all of the separate VP rules make it look like an accident that V is always at the left of VP in English. This is because you could change the position of V in one of the rules without changing the others. So with the unconflated rules, there is no "general" claim about where V must appear. But if you change the position of V in the conflated VP rule, then all VPs would be affected. That is, this rule does make the general and likely correct claim that V has a single main position in any English VP, a claim that the unconflated rules fail to make because they keep every structural possibility separate. So the conflated rule form allows significant generalizations about where Vs go in all VPs, where Ns go in all NPs, etc. that otherwise could not be stated.

4.2   Infinity and Recursion

What we've seen thus far is that PS grammar has the ability in principle to account for (i) why the words line up as they do and (ii) what hierarchic structure a given sentence should be assigned. However, we have not yet explained the infinity property – why is it that there are not just a lot of possible sentences but infinitely many possible sentences? The answer lies in the mathematical notion **recursion**.

To begin, let's consider what might at first glance seem to be an unrelated problem – describing the structure of NPs such as the underlined one in (13):

(13)   <u>A book in our library</u> discusses flying saucers.

A proform test indicates that this sequence is indeed an NP, since it can be replaced by a ProNP, as in (14a) or coordinated with another NP as in (14b):

(14)   a. <u>It</u> discusses flying saucers.
      b. <u>A book in our library</u> and <u>a new DVD</u> discuss flying saucers.

By inspection, *in the library* is a PP. (Tests of constituency easily verify this.) Further, there is evidence to indicate that the sub-sequence *a book* also forms its own phrase, an NP. For instance, this sequence can be replaced/referred to by a proform as in (15a) or coordinated with another NP as in (15b):

(15)   a. <u>A book</u> in our library and <u>one</u> on my shelf discuss flying saucers.
      b. <u>A book</u> and a <u>new DVD</u> in our library discuss flying saucers.
                               (where both are in our library)

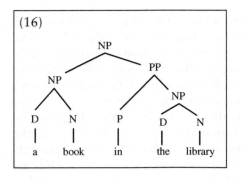

(16)

These results point to a structure such as (16), for which we don't yet have a rule.

Actually, the only part of the structure that is problematic is the top NP with its daughters NP and PP. We already have rules for the rest of the structure. We could remedy the situation by simply adding to grammar (2) the rule in (17), an easy and straightforward modification.

(17) NP → NP PP

This and the other rules of (2) would now give us tree (16).

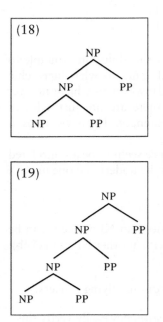

(18)

(19)

Taking care of this descriptive problem has a very welcome consequence – infinity! Rule 17 is a **recursive rule** – it can cycle indefinitely on its own output. If we applied rule 17 to the daughter NP of (17), we would get a partial structure like (18).

And applying it again, we could get tree (19). Are there indeed structures like this? Yes, as seen in (20a – b).

(20)   a. a book [PP in our library] [PP about flying saucers]
       b. a book [PP in our library] [PP about flying saucers] [PP with a tattered cover]

In fact, there is no largest NP of this sort. Rule (17) could be employed **recursively** as in (18) and (19) to produce an NP of any size. Since there is no largest such NP, the set of possible NPs (and the sentences containing them) is infinite. The answer to the infinity question appears to lie in the presence of recursive rules.

In fact, given that human language grammars are phrase-generation systems, it may be that in their simplest form, they must have infinite output. In order to block infinite output, you would have to disallow recursive rules like (17), and to do that, you would have to impose a special ban on rules having identical mothers and daughters, an extra complication. Without such a ban, we can have rules like (17). Also, as we shall soon see, there are cases of recursion that don't directly involve mothers and daughters, so such a ban wouldn't actually work to block recursion anyway. Thus the infinity property of languages may simply be a direct consequence of grammars being phrase-generating systems.

4.3   A Theory of Modification and Structural Ambiguity

Rule 17 is a rule of **adjunction**. It allows you to add PPs to an NP as **modifiers** – expressions that further describe the NP they attach to. With structures like (16), (18), and (19), we might start to develop certain aspects of our theory of grammar related to meaning – the **semantic** part of the system. Let's propose the following rule for determining what **adjunct PPs** in these structures modify.

(21)   **The modifier rule**
    A modifier (such as an adjunct PP) modifies its sister head phrase.

To explain a bit, in a tree like (16) (repeated here as (22)), the NP *a book* is a **phrasal head**.

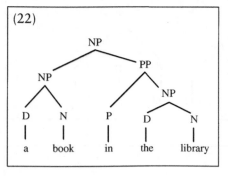

That is, it is the essential portion of the whole NP phrase and contains the **lexical head** *book*. The PP is "extra" – it is non-essential and omissible. It is the head that projects its category label N(P) to the top. So the rule in (21) says that the PP *in the library* should be understood as modifying its sister head phrase *a book*. Next, consider the structure in (23).

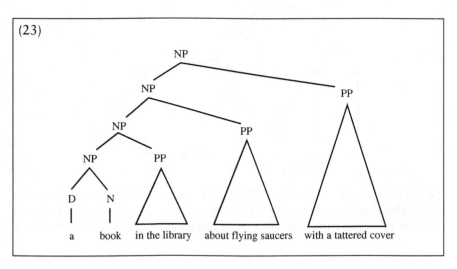

Applying the rule to this structure gives us the interpretation that the book is in the library, it concerns flying saucers, and it has a tattered cover.

What is even more interesting here are the consequences of the rule in (21) for NPs such as (24):

(24)   The box on the table with three legs.

This sentence has two possible meanings – either the table has three legs or the box does. What's really neat about the NP adjunction rule 17 and the modifier rule in (21) is that together they correctly predict this result! Sentence (24) has two possible structural analyses, (25) and (26).

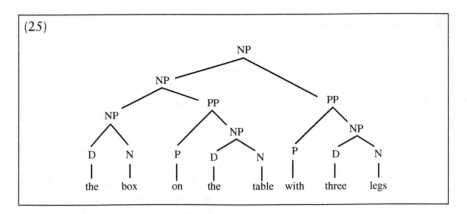

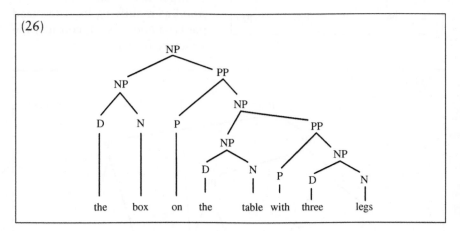

Following the rule in (21), tree (25) should mean that the box is on the table, and the box has three legs, and tree (26) should mean that the box is on the table, and the table has three legs. This is an instance of what is called **structural**

ambiguity – the situation where a word sequence has more than one possible structural analysis, which may lead to a semantic ambiguity such as this one. The fact that our theory accomplishes the analytic feat of explaining cases of structural ambiguity without any modification is **independent evidence** that our theory is on the right track as a model of C_{HL}/linguistic competence.

As a final note, it is interesting to consider how a child might "learn" a rule like the modifier rule. Considering the discussion in Chapter 1 of language acquisition, innateness, and the Principles & Parameters hypothesis, it is very unlikely that there is any direct evidence that would allow a child to learn the modifier rule from the available primary data. To the extent that this rule holds consistently within English and across languages, it thus seems plausible that it is a candidate for being a Principle – a "built-in" piece of knowledge for interpreting modifiers. Much more evidence is needed to pursue this possibility, but it is worth noting here.

4.4   Other Instances of Recursion

There are other instances of recursion, other places where the grammar can produce infinity. Parallel to NP adjunction is VP adjunction. As noted earlier in Chapter 3, *do so* is a ProVP. Thus, consider the sentences in (27) and tree (28):

(27)   a. Mary smoked a cigar in the morning, and ...
     b. ... Max did so in the evening.
     c. ... Max did so too.

The VP proform *did so* in (27b) refers to the word sequence *smoked a cigar* and hence indicates that this word sequence is a VP. *Did so* in (27c) refers to

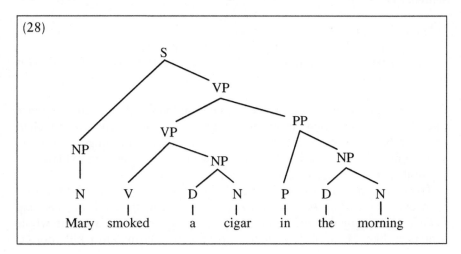
(28)

smoked a cigar in the morning and hence indicates that this word sequence is also a VP. Thus it appears that the sentence in (27a) contains two VPs, one nested inside the other, as in (28). Though the rule needed to create the VP-within-VP structure is not in the grammar thus far, it is easy to add as the rule in (29):

(29) VP → VP PP

This is clearly another recursive rule, in this case a rule of VP adjunction – one that adds "extra"/optional VP modifiers. Here too, we have the potential for creating infinitely many VPs, and hence infinitely many sentences containing them. Actually, the process of adjunction may be available for a range of different categories. The rules that we have dealt with so far are **category-specific** rules – rules that spell out the contents for specific categories. We might instead offer the possibility that adjunction is due to a **category-neutral** rule – one that can apply to a range of categories. As a first attempt, such a rule might look like the one in (30).

(30) XP → XP PP

If we take X in this rule to be a variable whose value might be N, V, or another appropriate category, then we would have a single general rule about the structure of adjunction. (It is understood that once we set the value of an X, then the other X in the structure must have the same value; that is, X here is a "bound" variable.) As we develop our theory of syntax, we will see a bit later that perhaps the entire grammatical system is category-neutral.

Another instance of recursion has to do with sentences. Consider the sentences in (31):

(31) a. Mary makes great pancakes.
      b. Max believes that Mary makes great pancakes.
      c. Zoe told Hermione that Max believes that Mary makes great pancakes.

As was noted earlier, and what we see again in (31), is that given a sentence like (31a), you can extend it by making it part of another sentence, which in turn can be extended in this way, etc. Again, there is no longest sentence, so sentences again go infinite. Here too, we lack the rule(s) to explain this possibility, but they aren't hard to add.

To create a first approximation of the needed rule, consider the fact that verb expressions like *believe* and *tell someone* can take NP objects, e.g. *believe the rumor* or *tell someone the story*. Thus it appears that whole sentences like *Mary makes great pancakes* are getting into NP (object) position. We might say that there is a rule like the one in (32) that allows this possibility:

(32) NP → Comp S

Here, Comp(lementizer) is the lexical category for words like *that* which accompany such NP-positioned sentences – sentences acting as subjects or objects in other sentences. With this rule, our theory of syntax can assign structures like those in (33) and (34) to these sentences.

The sort of recursion that we see here is not due to the form of one rule per se, but instead is due to the fact that S introduces NPs that can in turn reintroduce S into the structure. It is hard to see how such recursion could easily be blocked, so we can conclude that recursion/infinity is virtually unavoidable in systems such as these – such systems naturally go infinite.

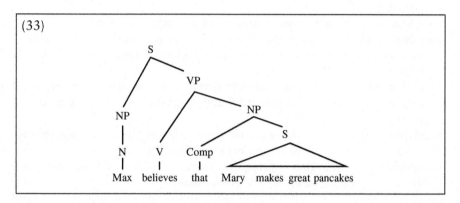

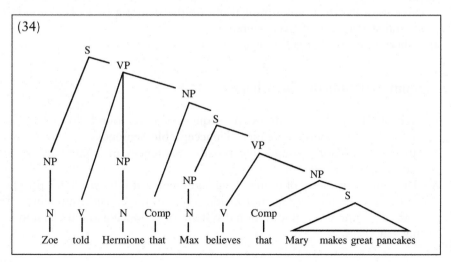

4.5   Some Summary Terms

The terms to follow are basic to the syntax of complex sentences – sentences containing other sentences. These will prove useful in further analyzing sentence structure:

recursive category: a syntactic category that may dominate/contain other instances of itself in a syntactic structure

recursive grammar/system: a grammar that contains recursive rules/categories; a system that may (in theory) cycle indefinitely on its own output

recursion: the quality/property of being recursive

embedded S: a sentence that is contained within, and functions as a part of, another sentence

matrix S: a sentence that contains another sentence functioning as a proper part of it

root S: a sentence that is not contained in any other sentence

linguistic creativity: a speaker's ability to produce/understand "novel" utterances; a speaker's ability to produce/understand any of infinitely many well-formed sentences

head (lexical): the central lexical item within a phrase; the lexical item that a phrase is built around; the word that dictates the type of the immediately surrounding phrase

head (phrasal): the central/core phrase within a larger phrase; the main phrase containing the lexical head and projected from it

complement: a phrase that is a (required) sister of the lexical head of another phrase (the complements of a V are its sisters)

adjunct: a phrase (often PP) whose sister and mother are identical phrasal categories; in effect, any optional phrase that is not a part of the fundamental structure of a given sentence

modifier: a phrase that is the sister of a lexical or phrasal head

Summary Points of This Chapter

- **Acceptable** sentences are word sequences that sound "natural" as sentences to a native speaker. **Unacceptable** sentences are word sequences that don't sound like possible sentences in a language to a native speaker.
- The infinity property of human languages makes it impossible for people to learn a language by memorization, imitation, etc. They must instead learn a **grammar**, a computational system for producing and understanding sentences.

- Since such **grammars are completely subconscious,** we can't observe them directly. To try to discover their contents, we can begin to "model" a grammar by creating a system (i) that successfully predicts which word sequences are "acceptable" sentences and which ones are not, (ii) that assigns "correct" structure to acceptable sentences, and (iii) that explains the infinity property of human language.
- **Phrase structure (PS) rules** offer a promising start in being able to address all of the above aspects of the real, subconscious grammar.
- By adding a **theory of modification,** PS rules are further capable of explaining aspects of what sentences mean and how certain phrases or sentences may have more than one meaning – instances of **structural ambiguity.**

Supplementary Notes and Problems

Notes on PS rules

The system of PS rules arrived at in this chapter looks as follows:

Unconflated form: Conflated form:

1 S → NP VP
2 S → NP Aux VP   rules 1–2:   S → NP (Aux) VP
3 VP → V
4 VP → V NP
5 VP → V PP   rules 3–9: $VP \rightarrow V \ (NP) \left(\left\{ \begin{array}{c} NP \\ PP \\ AjP \end{array} \right\} \right)$
6 VP → V AjP
7 VP → V NP NP
8 VP → V NP PP   (These basic VP rules reflect the various
9 VP → V NP AjP   transitivity possibilities.)
10 PP → P NP
11 NP → N
12 NP → D N
13 NP → AjP N
14 NP → D AjP N   rules 11–14:   NP → (D) (AjP) N
15 AjP → Aj
16 AjP → Int Aj   rules 15–16:   AjP → (Int) Aj

Recursive rules:
17 NP → NP PP   (NP adjunction)
18 NP → Comp S   (sentence recursion)
19 VP → VP PP   (VP adjunction)

Problems

1. Non-recursive structures. Using PS rules 1–16 above, draw trees that these rules allow ("predict") for each of the following sentences:
   a. The reporter won a very important prize.
   b. The Queen will award some guests knighthoods.
   c. Very fast cars can be quite expensive.
   d. The kids put some frogs in the pool.
   e. Max left.
   f. The quite entertained investigator smirked.

2. Discuss how applying tests of constituency to the sentences in problem 1 supports the correctness of the trees in problem 1 above.

3. Use the PS rules and the **theory of grammaticality** to explain why word sequence (a) is not a sentence of English but word sequence (b) is:
   a. the some pool in put frogs kids the
   b. the kids put some frogs in the pool

4. Recursive structures. Using all of the PS rules above, draw trees that these rules allow ("predict") for each of the following sentences:
   a. The pencil in your pocket has no lead.
   b. Jane thinks that Tarzan is in Berlin.
   c. The Queen has arrived in a carriage.
   d. Mary said that Laura thinks that George should buy a yacht.

5. (**Advanced**) Structural ambiguity. Draw trees and use the **modifier rule** to explain the following ambiguous structures:
   a. the box behind the door with no latch
   b. Bill made the bench in the garage.

5

Assigning Meaning in Sentences

If the modifier rule of the last chapter is any indication, there appear to be aspects of the meaning of sentences that are structure-based, that is, determined from syntactic structure. One key aspect of sentence meaning, **grammatical function (GF)**, has been conjectured by Chomsky and others also to be structure-based. We'll explore this idea and others related to sentence meaning here.

5.1 Grammatical Function and Sentence Meaning

GFs are the subject and object relations in a sentence – who is doing what to whom, etc., as illustrated in the sentences of (1):

(1) a. Mary gave Max a gift
    b. Max saw Mary.

In (1a), for example, *Mary* is the **subject** (an "**agent**" or "**doer**"), and *Max* and *a gift* are objects, or better, **complements**. *Max* is a **recipient** or **goal**, and *a gift* is a simple object or **theme**. In sentence (1b), *Max* is a subject, but here he hasn't done anything – rather he has experienced or perceived something, so he is an **experiencer**. Obviously, these semantic designations are key to the basic interpretation of any sentence. The question that we want to address here first is how meanings such as these get assigned to the particular parts of a sentence.

Syntactic Analysis: *The Basics*   Nicholas Sobin
© 2011 Nicholas Sobin

Let's refer to the subjects and objects of a sentence as its **arguments** (a term taken from predicate logic). Further, let's refer to the specific meanings of the arguments such as agent, experiencer, goal, etc. as "thematic roles," or better, **theta roles**. As seen in (1) above, the subjects of sentences, as well as the complements, vary in what theta roles they are assigned, depending on the verb. So in order to work out what the arguments of a sentence mean, that is, what theta role a given argument should be assigned, we'll first deal with the problem of identifying subjects and complements.

In the active sentences that we have considered thus far, the subject of a sentence reliably appears as the daughter of S and sister of VP, as in tree (2).

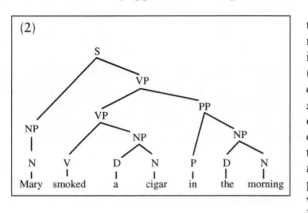

(2)

In (2), the NP *Mary* is the subject. The complement(s) of a verb is (are) its sister (or sisters). In (2), the NP *a cigar* is the complement (object) of *smoked*. Verbs aren't the only categories that take complements. Prepositions do too, so the NP *the morning* is the complement of *in*. Recall that whereas a complement is a sister of a lexical head, an adjunct is the sister of a phrasal head. In (2), the PP *in the morning* is an adjunct. Verbs don't assign theta roles to adjuncts, but they do assign theta roles to their arguments (their subject and complement(s)).

As a first approximation, let's say, then, that we have the system in (3) for determining the GF of each argument in a sentence.

(3)   **Grammatical functions based on "local" structural configuration**

   Subject function
   An NP is a **subject** if it is the daughter of S and a sister of VP

   Complement function (objects, etc.)
   Any phrase (XP) is a **complement** if it is a daughter of a VP or PP and a sister of V or P, respectively.

Once we can identify subjects and complements, we can assign the theta roles of a given verb.

Before turning to theta role assignment, we can say a bit more about adjuncts. We can identify the general function of an adjunct by how it is built into the sentence. In additon to (2) above, consider the tree in (4).

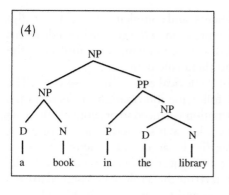

(4)

In (4), the adjunct PP is built into an NP, and has an **adjectival** function – it helps designate which book is being referred to. In (2) above, the adjunct PP is built into a VP and has an **adverbial** function – in this case it designates when something happened. Adverbial modifiers carry information concerning "when" or "where" or "how" or "why," whereas adjectival modifiers designate "which one(s)." We might codify this in an interpretive rule such as (5):

(5) **Adjunct function**

An adjunct XP is **adjectival** if it is a daughter of an NP and sister of an NP.

An adjunct XP is **adverbial** if it is a daughter of a VP and sister of a VP.

Rule (5) refers to XP (any phrasal category) rather than PP, since in fact adjuncts come from a variety of categories, including NP (e.g. *yesterday*, *last night*), AjP, and AvP (e.g. *very quietly*). This rule would correctly identify/ interpret the PP in (2) as "adverbial," and the PP in (4) as "adjectival."

5.2 Theta Roles and Argument Structure

Now that we have a way of determining the various grammatical functions (subject or complement) of the arguments in a sentence, we can deal more explicitly with the question of theta role assignment. Consideration of the sentences in (6) offers some clues as to how we should proceed.

(6) a. Mary put a motorcycle in the garage.
b. Mary washed a motorcycle in the garage.

Sentence (6a) is unambiguous. It has only one meaning. However, sentence (6b) is ambiguous – it has two distinct meanings. The expression *in the garage* might mean which motorcycle (but not where she washed it), or it might mean where she washed a motorcycle (but not which one). Further, this expression is omissible in (6b), but not in (6a), as illustrated in (7):

(7) a. *Mary put a motorcycle.
b. Mary washed a motorcycle.

Since adjuncts are extra, omissible elements, and complements are (normally) required elements, it appears that the expression *in the garage* has a different status in the two sentences. Since verbs select complements, it looks like the two verbs here make different GF and theta role demands.

Let's deal with these facts in terms of the lexical entries for these verbs. The lexical entry for a verb will carry the following information: (i) its **form** (its phonological representation – the information you need to pronounce it); (ii) its own lexical **category** (V – that's how we know it's a verb); (iii) its meaning (which we won't try to replicate here); (iv) its **argument structure** (the enumeration of the arguments (the subject and object(s)) that it requires); (v) the syntactic **category of each argument**; and (vi) the **theta role to be assigned to each argument**. Sample lexical entries for *wash* and *put* are given in (8) and (9):

(8) *wash*, V, . . ., Args: Cats: Theta roles:
                        1   NP   agent
                        2   NP   theme

(9) *put*, V, . . .,   Args: Cats: Theta roles:
                        1   NP   agent
                        2   NP   theme
                        3   PP   location

Let's understand the "1" argument to always be "subject," the "2" argument to be "first complement," and the "3" argument to be "second complement." So lexical entry (8) says that *wash* must be in a sentence with a subject NP and one complement NP, which are assigned the theta roles "agent" and "theme," respectively. Lexical entry (9) says that *put* must be in a sentence with an NP subject, and two complements, the first an NP, and the second, a PP. It will assign these three arguments the theta roles "agent," "theme," and "location," respectively, as in (10). Such information within a lexical

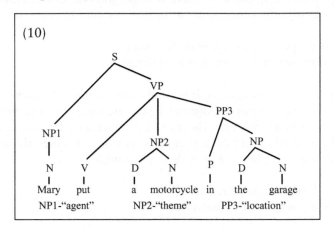

entry about the arguments required, their category, and the theta roles that they are to be assigned is referred to as a **theta grid**.

Now we can produce an explanation of why sentence (6b), but not (6a), is ambiguous, why the PP in (6b) is omissible, and why the interpretation of the PP in (6b) when present is ambiguous. The lexical information for *put* requires us to analyze sentence (6a) as in (10). The numbers in (8) and (9) indicate GF, and based on GFs, these NPs are assigned theta roles by the verb. With *put*, only one structural analysis is possible, so there is no ambiguity. However, with *wash*, two analyses are possible, since *wash* makes no use of the PP. Thus the PP is free to be an adjunct (in fact, that's all it can be here), and in this case it might be either a VP adjunct or an NP adjunct, as seen in (11) and (12), respectively.

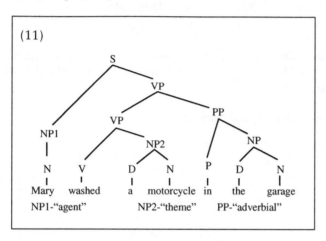

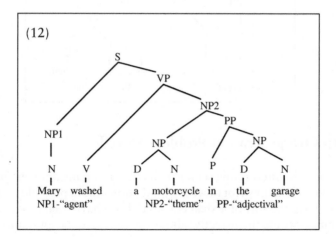

We might say that such a sentence with *wash* cannot be assigned a structure like (10) – that would violate the following rule about theta role assignment, known as the **Theta Criterion**:

(13)   **The Theta Criterion**
       Each argument must be assigned one (and only one) theta role, and each
       theta role must be assigned to one (and only one) argument.

That is, a verb must have all and only the arguments specified in its theta grid. Anything else must be analyzed as an adjunct. The lexical entry for an intransitive verb would look like the one for *smile* in (14):

(14)   *smile*, V,..., Args :   Cats :   Theta roles :
                          1   NP   agent

That is, intransitive verbs like this cannot license a complement. So a sentence like (15) would be assigned a structure like (16), where V is the sole daughter of its mother VP.

(15)   Mary arrived at the station.

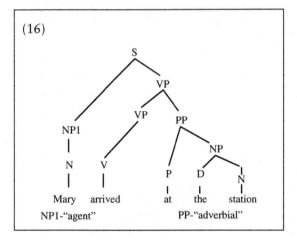

5.3   An Overgeneration Problem Solved

This approach to interpreting sentences has a very significant benefit. It saves the theory from making a lot of wrong predictions about possible sentences. If we did not have the sort of lexical entries that we have been discussing, then the grammar would incorrectly allow any verb to be put into any VP structure, incorrectly allowing many sentences that are clearly bad ones, as exemplified in (17):

(17)   a. *Mary smiled the cat.
       b. *Mary put the book.
       c. *Mary adores.

In fact, if the grammar could not restrict where particular verbs go, then we would have a massive problem of **overgeneration** – the situation in which the theory predicts more sentences (in this case, many more) to be possible than actually are possible. But this problem is greatly reduced with the introduction of argument structure into lexical entries – a verb can only head a VP that its lexical entry/argument structure specifies.

Summary Points of This Chapter

- The **grammatical function** of the arguments and adjuncts in a sentence can be determined from their structural positions.
- The lexical entry for a verb includes a **theta grid** – information about (i) the **arguments** (subject and complements) that the verb requires, the **syntactic category** of each argument, and the **theta role** that is to be assigned to each argument.
- An adjunct has an **adverbial** function if it is adjoined to a VP, and an **adjectival** function if it is adjoined to an NP.
- In many instances, theta grids are key to predicting whether or not a given sentence is **structurally ambiguous**.
- Theta grids are key to solving the problem of placing verbs in the appropriate VP structure, solving what would otherwise be a massive **overgeneration** problem.

Problems

1. Following the model of trees (10), (11), (12), and (16) in this chapter, draw trees with the correct theta roles and adjunct functions for each of the following sentences. Relevant argument structures are given below:

   a. Mary placed the lamp on the table.
   b. The lamp on the table was quite expensive.
   c. Mary arrived at the station.
   d. The in-laws arrived at the station at 5 p.m. (meaning: they arrived at 5 p.m.)

place, V, ...,	Args:	Cats:	Theta roles:
	1	NP	agent
	2	NP	theme
	3	PP	location

be, V, ...,	Args:	Cats:	Theta roles:
	1	NP	entity
	2	NP/AjP/PP	quality

("NP/AjP/PP" means the complement may be NP, AjP, or PP)

arrive, V, ...,	Args:	Cats:	Theta roles:
	1	NP	experiencer

2. Use trees with theta roles and adjunct functions to explain the structural ambiguity in the following sentences:

a. Mary wanted the lamp on the table.
b. The officials at the station said that Mary left at 5 p.m.
c. Mary put the lock on the table by the window.

want, V, ...,	Args:	Cats:	Theta roles:
	1	NP	experiencer
	2	NP	theme

say, V, ...,	Args:	Cats:	Theta roles:
	1	NP	agent
	2	NP	theme

leave, V, ...,	Args:	Cats:	Theta roles:
	1	NP	agent
	(2	NP	theme)

("(2...)" means a complement NP is "optional" with *leave*)

put, V, ...,	Args:	Cats:	Theta roles:
	1	NP	agent
	2	NP	theme
	3	PP	location

3. (**Advanced**) From what has been said about complements and adjuncts, use the sentences in each group below to determine what the theta grid should be for the verb used in that group.

   a. Mary likes the book.
      *Mary likes.
      Mary likes the book on the table.

   b. Mary laughed.
      *Mary laughed Bill.
      Mary laughed on Friday.
      Mary laughed on Friday at Bill.

   c. Mary gave a present to the doorman.
      *Mary gave a present.
      *Mary gave to doorman.
      Mary gave a present to the doorman at the north entrance.
      *Mary gave a present at/under/on/with/beside the doorman.

   d. *Mary expects.
      Mary expects a surprise.
      Mary expects that Max will arrive.

   e. *Mary said.
      *Mary said a joke.
      Mary said that Max will arrive.

   f. *Mary told.
      Mary told a joke.
      *Mary told that Max will arrive.
      Mary told Jane that Max will arrive.
      *Mary told a joke that Max will arrive.

4. (**Advanced**) Two (roughly) corresponding words in different languages may not have the same argument structure. For example, *put* strictly requires the two complements NP and PP, and neither of these can be omitted even in context, as in the following example.

   A: What was Mary doing with her purse?
   B: i. She put her money in her purse.
       ii. She put her money there.
      iii. *She put her money.
       iv. *She put.

In Spanish, the verb *meter* is often best translated as *put*; however, using *meter*, the same question may be answered in Spanish as follows.

C: v.   Ella metió el dinero en la bolsa.
          She put the money in the purse
          'She put her money in her purse'
     vi. Ella metió el dinero.
     vii. *Ella metió.

Considering these possible answers,

   a. what is the argument structure of *meter*, and
   b. what is the likely status in terms of grammatical function of locative expressions such as *en la bolsa* relative to *meter*?

6

Some Category-Neutral Processes

The theory of grammar that we have developed thus far is for the most part composed of **category-specific rules** – rules tuned to spelling out the contents of specific categories. The rules for NP look very different from those for VP or AjP, for instance. However, if the adjunction rules that we considered earlier are any indication, there may exist **category-neutral rules** – ones that apply to a range of categories, or perhaps to any category. Here, we'll consider a couple of what are clearly category-neutral rules, coordination and proform insertion. As our theory of syntax develops further, we will see that it is possible and even likely that all of the rules of syntax are category-neutral.

6.1   Coordination

Recall that one of our tests of phrasehood is the ability of a word sequence to participate in coordination – to be able to be joined to another word sequence with *and* or *or*, as in (1):

(1)   a. <u>The boy</u> and <u>the girl</u> arrived early.
      b. Mary <u>mowed the lawn</u> and <u>watered the flowers</u>.
      c. I put the tools <u>on the table</u> or <u>in the drawer</u>.

As noted earlier, coordination requires that the participating elements be of the same type. Thus, (1a) shows coordinated NPs, (1b) shows coordinated VPs, and (1c) shows coordinated PPs. Trying to cross-coordinate among these categories leads to ungrammaticality, as in (2):

Syntactic Analysis: *The Basics*   Nicholas Sobin
© 2011 Nicholas Sobin

(2)   a. *the boy and watered the grass
      b. *mowed the lawn and in the drawer

Not only must the coordinated elements be identical, but the whole coordinate structure itself appears also to be a phrase of the same type as its daughter elements. Thus, just as *the boy* in (1a) is evidenced to be an NP by its ability to be replaced by the ProNP *he*, the complete coordinate structure *the boy and the girl* also appears to be an NP, as evidenced by its ability to be replaced by the ProNP *they*.

The same is true of the VP coordination in (1b) and the PP coordination in (1c). Just as a simple VP might be referred to by the ProVP *do so* (e.g. *Bill watered some flowers and Mary did so too*), so too can a coordination of VPs be targeted by *do so*, as in (3):

(3)   Mary bought a car and drove to St Louis, and Max did so too.

Coordinated PPs can also be targeted by a single proform, as in (4):

(4)   Max works out in the morning and in the afternoon, and Mary works out then too:

Thus it appears that there is a single strategy for creating coordinate structures that applies to any category. This generalization could not be captured in category-specific rules such as those in (5):

(5)   a. NP → NP Conj NP
      b. VP → VP Conj VP
      c. etc.   (where Conj is the lexical category for *and* and *or*)

Such a repetitive characterization allows the possibility that coordination might somehow be altered for one category but not another, missing the generalization that all coordination necessarily works the same way. However, a category-neutral rule such as (6) succeeds in capturing the notion that all coordinations of the sort discussed here must work according to the same rule.

(6)   X → X Conj X (where X = any phrasal or lexical category)

Here, we understand the Xs to be **bound variables** – that is, when the rule is employed, all Xs must be given identical values. Thus the rule will produce coordinate structures as seen in (7) and (8). Any structures involving mismatched categories are disallowed by rule (6).

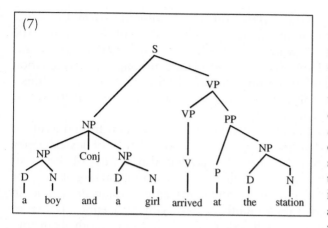

There is a logic to this. What coordination such as that exemplified here allows you to do is to take more than one constituent such as *a boy* and *a girl* and create from these a single constituent that will fit directly into the positions already made available by the other rules of the grammatical system. A mismatch of categories would leave the mother category of the coordination indeterminate.

The discussion to this point has dealt with the coordination of phrases. However, as noted in rule (6), coordination appears to apply to both phrases and single lexical items. Some examples of single-word coordination are the following:

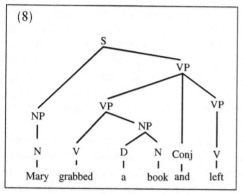

(9) a. A <u>boy and girl</u> are at the door. (N coordination)
     b. Mary <u>trimmed and watered</u> the hedge. (V coordination)
     c. The wrench is <u>on or near</u> the work bench. (P coordination)

Further, the following coordinations are not possible:

(10) a. *A <u>boy and girls</u> are at the door.
       (cf. A boy and some girls are at the door.)
     b. *Mary <u>put and painted</u> the chair on the work bench.
       (c.f. Mary put the chair on the work bench, and painted it (there).)

Noun coordinations like (9a/10a) display a number of striking features. The first is that the coordinated nouns appear to have to be of the same "number" (singular or plural). Thus both nouns in (9a) are singular, and the number mismatch in (10a) renders the coordination ungrammatical. Second, although you can't normally use a singular common count noun like *girl* alone in an NP (e.g. *[ₙₚ *Girl*] *is at the door*), "girl" without its own determiner in (9a) does not lead to ungrammaticality, and it is somehow understood to be using the determiner "a" which is to the left of "boy." ((9a) clearly means "*a boy and a̲ girl...*") How is this possible? Third, although the coordination in (9a) forms a plural reference, only singular determiners such as "a," "this," or "that" may be used in (9a), and not plural determiners like "these" or "those" (e.g. *These boy and girl...*).

A possible explanation of these facts comes in large part from the rule of coordination itself. It is possible that the coordination of lexical items requires not only identity of category type, but also identity of certain of the lexical features that are key to that lexical item interacting with other immediate elements. For instance, a noun must agree with its determiner in number. If coordination forms a mother category that is identical to that of its daughters, the coordination of lexical nouns will form a mother category noun (not NP). Further, nouns must select a determiner, so the mother category noun must have the necessary features to do so. Since these are determined from the words being coordinated, the key features will all have to match, as otherwise there would be no way to decide what the needed features for the mother category are, just as in the case of matching category. So the coordination of two singular nouns results in the creation of a singular mother noun, and the matching determiner will necessarily be singular. This is illustrated in (11).

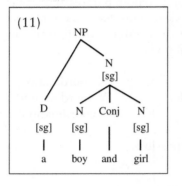

In the case of verb coordination, the coordinated verbs must have compatible argument structures so that the "super" verb that is created by verb coordination will know how to select its complements, etc. Thus, (9b) is a viable verb coordination, since both the verbs involved (*trim* and *water*) are single-complement-taking verbs, and the attempted coordination in (10b) is ungrammatical because the argument structures of the two verbs involved (*put* and *paint*) are fundamentally different.

As a final note, here while the subject NP in (9a) is internally singular, the agreeing verb form ("are") is plural. Agreement of subject and verb does not directly involve the lexical category N, but instead NP. So it appears that the number characteristic of the NP for purposes such as subject–verb agreement and proform reference (*a boy and girl* = *they/them*) may be determined differently from the NP-internal number features utilized in coordination. This is a large topic, and there is much more to be said about this.

6.2   Proform Insertion

Next, consider how proforms are inserted into a structure. As argued earlier, they appear to work consistently across all category types: proforms appear in phrasal positions. We might capture this notion in a single category-neutral rule such as (12):

(12)   XP → ProXP (where XP = any phrasal category)

Here, XP is a bound variable ranging over phrases, so if NP is the mother category, then following rule (12), its daughter must be ProNP. If the mother is VP, then the daughter must be ProVP. Assume that ProNP, ProVP, etc. are lexical categories, as mapped out in (13):

(13)   Sample lexicon of proforms

>   *she*, ProNP, …
>   *he*, ProNP, …
>   *I*, ProNP, …
>   *they*, ProNP, …
>   *her*, ProNP, …
>   etc.
>   *do so*, ProVP, …
>   *so*, ProAjP, …
>   *then*, ProPP, …
>   *there*, ProPP, …

Rule (12) and lexical entries such as those in (13) give structures such as those in (14) and (15).

As with coordination, rule (12) and the lexical entries of (13) work in concert with the rest of the system that we have developed thus far. There is a lot more of the system to be developed, but to this point, we have a system that

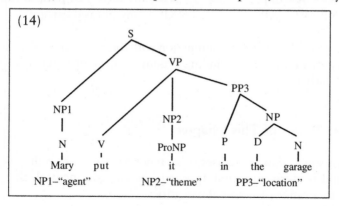

(14)

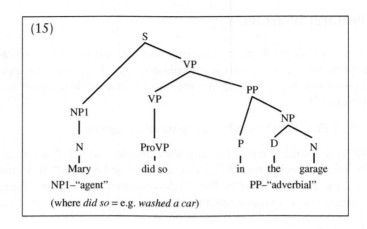

(15)

(where *did so* = e.g. *washed a car*)

is very successful as a first approximation of an English speaker's internalized system of grammar. Rule set (16) gives a summary of the phrase structure grammar that we have developed to this point:

(16)   **Summary PS rules**

$$S \rightarrow NP \ (Aux) \ VP$$

$$VP \rightarrow V \ (NP) \ \left(\left\{ \begin{array}{c} NP \\ PP \\ AjP \end{array} \right\} \right)$$

$$PP \rightarrow P \ NP$$
$$NP \rightarrow (D) \ (AjP) \ N$$
$NP \rightarrow Comp \ S$ (sentence recursion)
$$AjP \rightarrow (Int) \ Aj$$
$XP \rightarrow XP \ PP$ (adjunction; "XP" = any phrasal category)
$X \rightarrow X \ Conj \ X$ ("X" = any lexical or phrasal category)
$XP \rightarrow ProXP$ ("XP" = any phrasal category)

This system of rules works in conjunction with the theory of modification and the theory of the lexicon including argument structure and theta roles as discussed earlier.

Summary Points of This Chapter

- At least some of the processes of sentence formation including coordination and proform insertion appear to be **category-neutral**; that is, they apply to a range of different categories.

- **Coordination** is restricted to unifying two syntactic elements (lexical or phrasal) of the same type, and it produces a mother category of a type identical to that of its daughters.
- **Lexical coordination** involves the identity of not only the category label but also of certain lexical features key to selecting other immediate interacting elements of the sentence.
- **Proform insertion** also appears to be a category-neutral process restricted to phrases.
- Since **category-neutral rules are more general and economical** than category specific rules, the presence of some category-neutral processes points us toward exploring the question of whether more and perhaps all of the sentence formation rules/processes might be category-neutral rather than category-specific.

Problems

We have added rules for **coordination** and **proform insertion** to the rule system. For problems 1–4 below, draw the tree for each sentence. New relevant argument structures are added below.
Ones given earlier are not repeated.

1. Phrasal coordinations:
   a. <u>Mary and the boys</u> were playing in the garden.
   b. Mary <u>watered the flowers and mowed the grass</u>.
   c. Mary put the tools <u>in the box or on the shelf</u>.
   d. <u>Spies were creeping past the tent, and the guards heard them</u>.
   e. Mary is <u>smart and quite clever</u>.
   f. <u>Mary or Max</u> brought <u>a hammer and a drill</u>.
   g. Mary will arrive <u>on Tuesday or on Wednesday</u>.

2. Lexical coordinations:
   a. That <u>boy and girl</u> play soccer.
   b. Mary <u>bought and sold</u> a flute.
   c. The very <u>smart and clever</u> soloist smiled.
   d. Mary put the tools <u>on or under</u> the bench.

3. Proform substitution:
   a. <u>She</u> put the tools on the bench.
   b. Mary put <u>them</u> on the bench.
   c. Mary put the tools <u>there</u>.
   d. Mary bought apples and Jane <u>did so</u> too.
   e. <u>She</u> put <u>them</u> <u>there</u>.

4. (**Advanced**) Coordinations and proforms:

   a. Mary and I might buy a car or a truck.
   b. We bought and ate two cheeseburgers.
   c. I bought a book on Tuesday, and Mary did so on Wednesday.
      (Here, treat the PPs as adverbials; also, treat <u>did so</u> as a single proform.)
   d. Bill says that he writes novels, and Mary doesn't believe it.
      (Here, treat <u>doesn't</u> as Aux; also, <u>it</u> refers to the word sequence <u>that he writes novels</u>.)
   e. Spies were creeping past the tent, and we heard them.

play, V, ...,	Args:	Cats:	Theta roles:
	1	NP	agent
	(2	NP	theme)

water, V, ...,	Args:	Cats:	Theta roles:
	1	NP	agent
	2	NP	theme

mow, V, ...,	Args:	Cats:	Theta roles:
	1	NP	agent
	2	NP	theme

creep, V, ...,	Args:	Cats:	Theta roles:
	1	NP	agent

hear, V, ...,	Args:	Cats:	Theta roles:
	1	NP	experiencer
	2	NP	theme

buy, V, ...,	Args:	Cats:	Theta roles:
	1	NP	agent
	2	NP	theme

sell, V, ...,	Args:	Cats:	Theta roles:
	1	NP	agent
	2	NP	theme

eat, V, ...,	Args:	Cats:	Theta roles:
	1	NP	agent
	(2	NP	theme)

believe, V, ...,	Args:	Cats:	Theta roles:
	1	NP	agent
	2	NP	theme

5. (**Advanced**) If we treated coordination as category-specific rather than category-neutral, how many rules of coordination would there be? Assuming the grammatical system that we have developed thus far, give a list of these rules. Briefly explain the advantages of the category-neutral analysis.

7

How Structure Affects Pronoun Reference

In Chapter 3, we discussed some key relationships among the constituents of a tree. One of these was **dominates** – a constituent X dominates another constituent Y if and only if ("iff" in logic shorthand) there is a downward path of branches from X to Y. This is the basic "contains"/"consists of" relationship. The notion that a constituent in a tree contains other lexical or phrasal constituents is basic to the whole notion of PS grammar. Another key relation is **immediately dominates** – a constituent X immediately dominates another constituent Y iff X dominates Y and is connected to it by a single branch. This relation is central to PS rules. The PS rules embody all of the immediate dominance relations among the constituents. Recall that a constituent that immediately dominates another is the **mother,** and the constituents that are immediately dominated are its **daughters.** Constituents with the same mother are **sisters.**

Another relation among constituents that has proved key is one called **constituent command,** or more simply, **c-command.** It strongly involves the relation sister. A definition is given in (1):

(1) **C-command**
A constituent X *c-commands* another constituent Y and everything in (dominated by) Y iff X and Y are sisters.
(Or: X *c-commands* Y iff every constituent that dominates X also dominates Y.)

Put in the simplest terms, any constituent c-commands its sister constituent (or constituents), and everything that the sister constituent contains. To illustrate, consider the tree in (2).

Syntactic Analysis: *The Basics*   Nicholas Sobin
© 2011 Nicholas Sobin

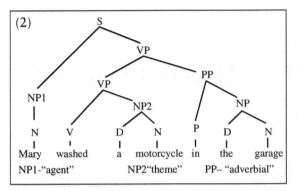

(2)

NP1-"agent"	
	NP2"theme"
	PP– "adverbial"

Mary washed a motorcycle in the garage

In (2), V c-commands NP2 and its daughters D and N. The lower VP c-commands PP and all of its contents. Likewise, PP c-commands the lower VP and all of its contents. NP1 c-commands the higher VP and everything in it. We can refer to the set of constituents that are c-commanded by some other constituent X as its **c-command domain,** which we define in (3):

(3)   **C-command domain of X**
      The *c-command domain* of X is comprised of the X's sister(s) and all of the constituents dominated by X's sister(s).

7.1   Negative Polarity Items (NPIs)

One area in which c-command appears to play a central role is in the use of **negative polarity items (NPIs)** – lexical expressions that appear in negative constructions but not in affirmative declarative constructions. NPIs include expressions such as *any, ever,* and *a red cent.* Such expressions only appear in negative sentences, most commonly, sentences with *not,* as in (4):

(4)   a. I didn't have <u>any</u> money. (but, *I had <u>any</u> money)
      b. I don't believe that Mary has <u>ever</u> had money
         (but, *I believe that Mary has <u>ever</u> had money)
      c. The treasure hunters didn't find <u>a red cent</u>.
         (but, *The treasure hunters found <u>a red cent</u>)

Examples such as (5) point to there being a condition on the appearance of NPIs in addition to the required presence of a negative element:

(5)   a. No hunters found <u>any</u> deer.
      b. The hunters didn't find <u>any</u> deer.
      c. *<u>Any</u> hunters found no deer.
      d. No one <u>ever</u> sees <u>any</u>thing.
      e. *<u>Any</u>thing is <u>ever</u> seen by no one.

The partial structure of (5a–c) is given in (6).

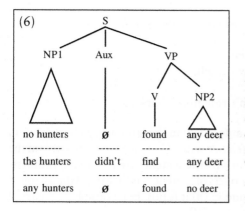

(6)

	no hunters	ø	found	any deer
	the hunters	didn't	find	any deer
	any hunters	ø	found	no deer

It appears that in addition to simply being present, the negative element (here, the constituent containing *not*, *–n't*, or *no*) must c-command the NPI. In (5a), NP1 c-commands NP2, as does Aux in (5b). In (5c), the expression with *any* is not c-commanded by a negative expression, and the sentence is ungrammatical. The same is true of (5d–e). So it appears that c-command is a critical factor in validating NPIs.

7.2 Co-reference Relations/Binding Theory

Another area involving c-command is that of reference relations among nominal expressions. The core question here is this: when can two NP expressions refer to the same entity, and when can they not? We'll look at three different types of nominal expressions here: "reflexives" (e.g. *herself*), "pronominals" (e.g. *she*, *her*), and "referring nominals" (noun-based expressions, e.g. *the girl*, *Mary*).

7.2.1 Reflexives, or "anaphors"

Reflexive pronouns are commonly called **anaphors**. Consider the sentences with anaphors in (7):

(7) a. Mary$_i$ saw herself$_i$
b. Jane$_j$ told Zelda$_k$ stories about herself$_{j/k}$
c. You$_i$ could have hurt yourself$_i$
d. I$_i$ couldn't help myself$_i$

The subscript letters indicate some entity in the world (e.g. a person or thing) that the nominal is referring to. When two nominal expressions bear the same subscript letter, this indicates that both expressions are referring to the same entity. In (7a), *Mary* and *herself* are the same person. Interestingly, this must be true – *herself* in this sentence cannot refer to someone else. In (7b), as indicated by the indices on *herself*, this expression can refer either to *Jane* or *Zelda*, and it must refer to one or the other – it cannot be a reference to someone else. Sentences (7c) and (7d) illustrate other anaphors.

The sentences of (8) show cases where anaphors fail:

(8)   a. *Mary's_i brother saw herself_i
      b. *The brother of Mary_i saw herself_i
      c. *My_i mother saw myself_i
      d. Those pictures of you_i don't resemble yourself_i

It appears that anaphors require an **antecedent** in the sentence, a constituent in the sentence that they can share a reference with. That idea works to explain the sentences of (7), but it doesn't explain why the sentences in (8) are ungrammatical. A key distinction between the two sets of sentences is this: in (7) the anaphor is c-commanded by its antecedent, and in (8) it is not. For example, the partial structure of (7a) is (9), and that of (8b) is (10).

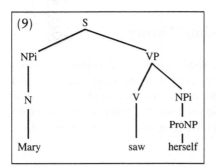

It is important to note here that the indices are not on the words but on the phrases that they head. In (9), the NP headed by *Mary* c-commands the NP headed by *herself*. In (10), it does not. It is the referential index of the phrasal head *the brother* that determines the index of the subject NP *the brother of Mary*. So *himself* would have been good in (10), as opposed to *herself*.

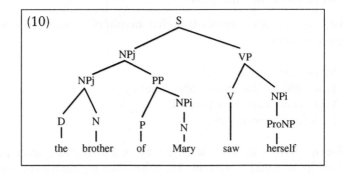

One more relevant fact about anaphors is that they must have a "local" antecedent, that is, the antecedent must be structurally close. A simplified version of this locality restriction is to say that the anaphor and its antecedent must be in the same clause (S). Thus sentences like (11) are ungrammatical because, although the antecedent c-commands the anaphor, these two constituents are in different clauses:

(11) *Mary$_i$ said that [Jake$_j$ saw herself$_i$]

Linguists utilize the term **binding** as characterized in (12) to account in more detail for how anaphors work:

(12) **Binding**
A constituent X *binds* another constituent Y iff X *c-commands* Y and X and Y are coindexed (co-referential).

That is, if X and Y refer to the same person or thing (bear the same index), and if X c-commands Y, then X is said to **bind** Y. Binding is used to state the rule that anaphors follow, a rule known as **Principle A**:

(13) **Principle A**
An *anaphor* (reflexive or reciprocal) must be "locally" bound (=bound in its clause).

Principle A applies in other languages as well. Consider the following German sentences:

(14) a. [$_S$ Maria$_i$ hat sich$_{i/*j}$ gesehen]
Maria has herself seen
"Maria saw herself"

b. [$_S$ Maria$_i$ glaubt daß [$_S$ Hedwig$_j$ sich$_{j/*k/*i}$ gesehen hat]]
Maria thinks that Hedwig herself seen has
"Maria thinks that Hedwig saw herself"

In German, as in English, the subject NP c-commands everything else in the sentence. *Sich* is the German reflexive pronoun for any gender. As with English reflexive pronouns, *sich* must be bound in its clause, as the sentences in (14) indicate.

7.2.2 Pronominals

Pronominals (ordinary non-reflexive ProNPs such as *her*, *him*, and *them*) almost mirror the behavior of anaphors. They involve c-command/binding in a negative way. In contrast to sentence (11), the same sentence, but with a pronominal (*her*) is fine, as in (15):

(15) Mary$_i$ said that [Jake$_j$ saw her$_{i/k}$]

Notice that *her* here could be *Mary* (co-indexed "i"), or it could be someone else (indexed "k"). In contrast to anaphors, pronominals display an

anti-locality effect. A pronominal cannot tolerate an antecedent that c-commands it within the clause. This is illustrated in (16):

(16)   *Mary$_i$ saw her$_i$

Sentence (16) cannot mean that Mary saw herself. It is only good if the *her* is someone else. The viable use of pronominals is encoded in what is termed **Principle B:**

(17)   **Principle B**
A pronominal cannot be "locally" bound (that is, it must be "free" in its clause).

Notice that, where an anaphor is bad because it is not c-commanded by its antecedent, as in (8b/10) above, this condition is fine for a pronominal, as seen in (18):

(18)   The brother of Mary$_i$ saw her$_i$

These are very striking facts. Everyone who speaks English knows these principles (known as the **Binding Principles**) subconsciously, yet they are never taught or spoken of, even in grammar books. There is evidence that children know them at a very early age. There is also some indication that other languages follow the same or similar principles. For example, pronominals in German appear to also follow Principle B in the following examples:

(19)   a. Maria$_i$ hat   sie$_{j/*j}$ gesehen
Maria   has   her   seen
"Maria saw her"

b. Maria$_i$ glaubt   daß   [Hedwig$_j$ sie$_{i/k/*j}$ gesehen   hat]
Maria   thinks   that   Hedwig   her   seen   has
"Maria thinks that Hedwig saw her"

In (19a), *sie* ('her'–a pronominal) can be any female except *Maria* – they are in the same clause, and *Maria* c-commands *sie*. In (19b), though *Maria* also c-commands *sie* here, they are not in the same clause, so *sie* can refer to *Maria* or to someone else, but not to *Hedwig*, which also c-commands *sie* and is in the same clause with it. So Principle B appears to work in German as it does in English.

7.2.3 Referring expressions

There is a third type of expression that does not tolerate a c-commanding antecedent anywhere in the structure. These expressions are the noun-based ones such as *Mary* or *the girl*. They are called "referring expressions," or simply **R-expressions**, because, unlike the pronoun-based expressions above, they do not need an antecedent to establish reference. They refer directly to someone or something in the world. For example, if someone says *Max saw her*, the listener has no way of knowing who *her* is, unless the referent has been overtly mentioned or pointed out earlier. Such a use of *her* is odd if there is no previous mention or indication of who *her* is supposed to refer to. That is, *her* requires an antecedent. But if someone says *Max saw Mary*, then the speaker is assuming that the listener knows who *Mary* is and that the term *Mary* is sufficient to identify who is being talked about without an antecedent. Hence, these noun-based expressions are called R(eferring) expressions.

R-expressions appear to obey a third Binding Principle, one also involving c-command, called **Principle C**. To see this, let's consider some data that show that R-expressions are distinct from both anaphors and pronominals. Consider the sentences in (20):

(20) a. [$_S$ She$_i$ saw Mary$_{j/*i}$]
      b. [$_S$ She$_i$ thinks that [$_S$ Max$_j$ saw Mary$_{k/*i/*j}$]]
      c. [$_S$ [$_{NP_j}$ [$_{PossP_i}$ Her] mother] loves Mary$_{i/k/*j}$]

Recall from our work with earlier structures that the subject NP c-commands VP and everything in VP (that is, everything else in the sentence). Hence the subject NP *she* in (20a) and (20b) c-commands the NP *Mary*. Note that in these sentences, *Mary* cannot refer to the c-commanding subject whether or not the c-commanding subject is in the same clause. Thus, sentence (20a) shows that R-expressions are different from anaphors, and (20) shows that R-expressions are different from pronominals. In (20c), the possessive phrase containing *her* does not c-command *Mary*, but the NP headed by *mother* does. Hence, *her* and *Mary* may have the same referent in (20c), but *her* and *mother* cannot. Facts such as these lead us to the following characterization of Principle C:

(21) **Principle C**
      An R-expression cannot be bound by another constituent anywhere in the sentence (that is, it must be "free" in the entire sentence).

Principle C governs the reference possibilities for R-expressions and thus explains why *Mary* cannot be co-referential with the subjects of the sentences in (20), or, for that matter, with any other constituent that c-commands it.

Again, German works like English in regard to these data, as seen in the sentences of (22):

(22)   a.   [$_S$ Sie$_i$ hat   Maria$_{j/*i}$ gesehen]
            She   has   Maria   seen
         "She saw Maria"

       b.   [$_S$ Sie$_i$ glaubt   daß   [$_S$ Hedwig$_j$ Maria$_{k/*i/*j}$ gesehen   hat]]
            She   thinks   that   Hedwig   Maria   seen   has
         "She thinks that Hedwig saw Maria"

       c.   [$_S$ [$_{NP_j}$ [$_{PossP_i}$ Ihr] Mutter]   liebt   Maria$_{i/k/*j}$]
            Her mother   loves   Mary

7.3   Acquiring the Binding Principles

Research has shown that children exhibit knowledge of these principles at a very early age. But how could children know such things early, and why would these principles be cross-linguistic? Recall here the discussion of the Principles & Parameters model of language acquisition discussed in Chapter 1. Principles A, B, and C, which are known together as the **Binding Principles,** and thought to constitute **Binding Theory,** have been considered by many as possible instances of innate principles. They are not "learned" from exposure to language, but appear to be hard-wired in human cognition. In this view, they are a part of the innate language endowment that every human brings to the task of acquiring a human language. A further indication that this might be so is that children are not exposed to the **negative data** discussed above – the facts about impossible binding constructions. That is, they don't appear to make mistakes in this realm and get corrected. This being the case, they lack the requisite negative evidence to formulate the Binding Principles solely through experience/learning, so many researchers conclude that these principles must have a strong basis in cognition. This discussion reflects one of the major questions facing any linguistic theory – which aspects of human language are "acquired" from exposure to language-specific data ("nurture"), and which aspects are innate ("nature")? We will have more to say about this as we further develop our theory of syntax.

Summary Points of This Chapter

- As with the earlier discussion of grammatical function and theta roles, syntactic structure appears to be a key factor in determining possible co-reference relations.
- Co-reference relations are licensed (allowed or disallowed) by the **Binding Principles A, B,** and **C,** which constitute the **Binding Theory.**
- **C-command** is a syntactic relationship that is central to each of the Binding Principles, as well as to other syntactic phenomena such as the distribution of negative polarity items.
- Since children exhibit early knowledge of Binding Theory, its principles may be instances of the innate/hard-wired principles that are thought to be a part of Universal Grammar, the innate initial language endowment that all humans possess.

Problems

1. Consider the following tree:

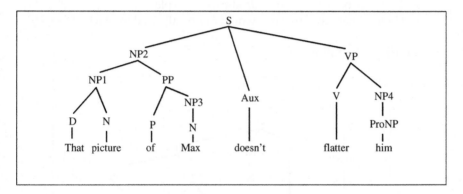

Answer each of the following questions:

    a. Which constituents does NP1 c-command?
    b. Which constituents does PP c-command?
    c. What constituent is in the scope of the modifier PP, and hence modified by it?
    d. Which constituents does NP2 c-command?
    e. Which constituents does V c-command?
    f. By which Binding Principle is *him* allowed ? Explain.
    g. By which Binding Principle would *himself* be disallowed? Explain.

2. Consider this tree:

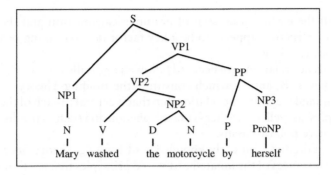

a. Which constituents does NP1 c-command?
b. Which constituents does PP c-command?
c. What constituent is in the scope of the modifier PP, and hence modified by it?
d. Which constituents are sisters of V, and hence qualify as its complements?
e. By what principle is *herself* allowed? Explain.
f. Under what circumstance would *her* be allowed in place of *herself*?

3. Consider the following tree:

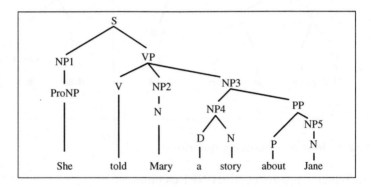

a. Which constituents does NP1 c-command?
b. Which Binding Principle is relevant to determining possible references for NP1?
c. Which binding Principle is relevant to determining possible references for NP2?
d. Which binding Principle is relevant to determining possible references for NP5?

e. Following the relevant Binding Principle, what are the reference possibilities for NP2?

f. Following the relevant Binding Principle, what are the reference possibilities for NP5?

4. Tree each of the following sentences and assign the appropriate theta roles and adjunct functions to the eligible NPs and PPs. Next, mark referential indices on NPs in accordance with the Binding Principles (one possible set only).

a. Mary put herself in a bad position.
b. Mary put her in a bad position.
c. The brother of Jack saw himself in the mirror.
d. The brother of Jack saw him in the mirror.
e. Jane said that Mary saw herself.
f. Jane said that Mary saw her.
g. Jane told Mary stories about herself.
h. She said that she saw Mary.

see, V, . . .,	Args:	Cats:	Theta roles:
	1	NP	experiencer
	2	NP	theme

tell, V, . . .,	Args:	Cats:	Theta roles:
	1	NP	agent
	2	NP	goal
	3	NP	theme

5. (**Advanced**) Answer each of the following:

a. Why can *her* in (4b) above not be *Mary*?
b. Why must *himself* in (4c) above be the brother and not Jack?
c. Why may *herself* in (4g) above be either *Jane* or *Mary*?
d. In the sentence *Mary said that she saw herself*, what is the relevant Binding Principle, and what are the reference possibilities for each of the three NPs *Mary*, *she*, and *herself*?

8

Complex Verb Forms

Although the theory of syntax that we've developed so far has quite a bit of empirical validity (that is, it makes quite a lot of good predictions (in fact, infinitely many) about possible and impossible sentences, and about the structure and meaning of the possible ones), it still suffers some fundamental inadequacies. For one thing, despite meeting the infinity requirement, it nonetheless massively **undergenerates**. That is, it is not yet capable of explaining why sentence (1a) below with its sequence of auxiliary verbs is possible, or how the interrogative proform *what* in (1b) is assigned an "object" meaning and why the verb *has* appears in front of the subject instead of behind it. We'll start to address these deficiencies in this chapter.

(1)   a. Mary might have been singing.
      b. What has Mary written?

8.1   Auxiliary Verbs and Recursive VP

The first deficiency we'll address is this: The grammar undergenerates sequences of auxiliary verbs, e.g. *She could have been swimming*. How should it be revised to allow for such verb sequences? Let's consider two competing hypotheses.

8.1.1 Two hypotheses

The first, the Complex Aux hypothesis, is given in (2):

(2) **Complex Aux hypothesis**

S → NP Aux VP

Aux → (M) (*have*) (*be*)

(M = *can, could, will, would, shall, should, may, might,* or *must*)

According to this hypothesis, the Aux element is not a lexical category, as we have treated it thus far, but is a more complex phrasal category, whose contents are a possible sequence of auxiliary verbs. **M(odal verb)** is any of the words: *can, could, will,* etc. as listed above in (2). Also, the auxiliary verbs *have* and *be* may occur following a modal in the order stated in the Aux rule of this hypothesis. Following this system, the sentence *Jane could have been eating tacos* would have the structure in (3).

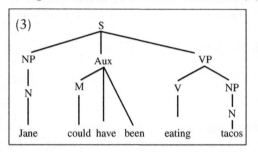

A second possible hypothesis about auxiliary verb sequences, the recursive VP hypothesis, is shown in (4). Like the Complex Aux hypothesis, this second hypothesis uses the category M as a lexical category with the same lexical membership. However, here there is no constituent Aux. Instead, the verbs *have* and *be* head their own VPs. Also, these verbs carry the feature [+ Aux], whereas "main" verbs (e.g. *eat*) are [−Aux].

(4) **Recursive VP hypothesis**

S → NP (M) VP

VP → V VP
   [+ Aux]

VP → V (NP) ({NP/PP/AjP})
   [−Aux]

   (M = *can, could,* etc.;

    V = *have* or *be*;

   [+ Aux]

   All "main" verbs (e.g. *swim*) are V   .)
                       [−Aux]

This hypothesis would analyze the sentence *Jane could have been eating tacos* as in (5).

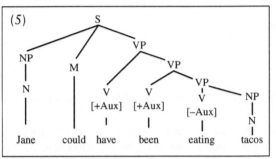

Here, we have VPs within VPs, so this is a "recursive" VP analysis. At first, it looks like the more complicated of the two hypotheses, but there is evidence that it is the better one.

8.1.2   Some decisive data

One phenomenon of relevance in deciding between these two hypotheses is "VP deletion." When a following sentence contains a VP that is identical to a VP of a preceding sentence, it (the redundant VP) may be omitted, as in (6):

(6)   Mary might [VP eat a taco], and Jane might [VP Ø] too.

In VP deletion, the whole VP must be omitted, and not just a verb or object NP, so (7a) and (7b) are not possible:

(7)   a. *Mary might eat a taco, and Jane might a cheeseburger.
      b. *Mary might eat a taco, and Jane might eat (too). (meaning "eat a cheeseburger")

Both of the preceding hypotheses could explain the VP deletion in (6), since in both hypotheses, the sequence V NP forms a VP. But now consider other instances of deletion such as in (8):

(8)   a. Mary could have been eating a taco, and Jane could have been eating a taco too.
      b. Mary could have been eating a taco, and Jane could have been ___ too.
      c. Mary could have been eating a taco, and Jane could have ___too.
      d. Mary could have been eating a taco, and Jane could ___ too.

Under both hypotheses, (8b), where the verb and its object have been deleted, is explainable as VP deletion. However, (8c) and (8d) are problematic for the Complex Aux analysis because the deleted sequences *been eating a taco* and *have been eating a taco* are not phrases under this analysis. We continue to assume, as we have from the start, that omissibility is exclusively a behavior of phrases – you can't just omit arbitrary word sequences. So whether we would attribute the deletion here to VP deletion or to some other deletion process, the Complex Aux analysis is in trouble with (8c) and (8d), since *only* phrases are omissible.

The recursive VP analysis fares very well here. Under this analysis, each of the deleted sequences is analyzed as a VP. Thus this analysis predicts that all of the deletions in (8) should be possible, and they are. So it looks like the recursive VP analysis is the way to go.

8.2   Verb Form

In dealing with auxiliary verbs, another problem presents itself – the problem of explaining the various forms that each verb takes. The forms being considered here are the inflectional forms that were discussed in Chapter 2. There we posited a rule of inflection that puts one of the possible inflectional suffixes onto a verb. But it isn't that simple. Syntactic context is a significant factor in which inflectional suffix is chosen. Consider a sentence such as (9):

(9)   She could have been swimming.

The verb after the modal *could* must be a bare/uninflected form. The verb after *have* must have the past participle suffix *-en/ed*. The verb after *be* must have the present participle suffix *-ing*. We can't scramble these endings, as (10) illustrates:

(10)   *She could having be swum.

As earlier, let's entertain two hypotheses about how these affixes are distributed.

8.2.1   The linear distribution hypothesis

One approach might be to try to lay out line by line in brute force fashion all of the possible sequences of verbs and suffixes, as in (11):

(11)   **Linear distribution**

> Aux → (Modal) have be -en V -ing
> (Modal) have V -en
> (Modal) be V -ing
> etc. (adding passive *be* makes this list much longer)

The Aux here is like the one from the earlier Complex Aux hypothesis. Problems arise immediately with this proposal. First, the sort of "Aux" architecture shown in (11) has already been rejected since it can't explain VP deletion. Second, there would have to be lots of specific rules to describe all of the possible verb-plus-inflection possibilities. Third, this analysis misses key generalizations such as the fact that a verb always takes past participle *-en/ed* when it is preceded by *have*. (That is, when you have to state such a combination more than once, then you haven't captured it as a single, necessary, general fact.)

8.2.2   The Affix Hopping hypothesis

A different possible approach is the one in (12):

(12)   **Affix Hopping**
   (i) [have -en] and [be -ing] are each single lexical entries. (That is, each of these lexical entries consists of two morphemes)
   (ii) there is a rule called "Affix Hopping" that says: When you encounter the sequence "affix – verb," then move the affix to the immediate right of that verb.

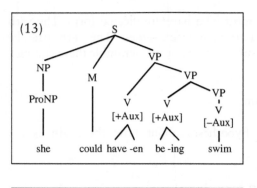

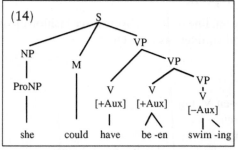

Under this analysis, the initial structure of sentence (9) would be tree (13).

Here, *-en* and *-ing* are affixes, and *have*, *be*, and *swim* are verbs. Thus, the affix – verb sequences are *-en be* and *-ing swim*. The sentence in (13) doesn't look like English yet, but if the rule Affix Hopping (AH) is applied to each of these affix–verb sequences, then (13) becomes (14).

In forming (14) from (13), each suffix has hopped onto the verb to its right. This gives us the right sequencing of morphemes, and it does so in a really interesting way. First, this analysis is compatible with the recursive VP analysis, the analysis argued for earlier. Second, this analysis requires only a single additional rule (AH), rather than a longer list of *ad hoc* rules stating each possible morpheme sequence. Third, this analysis captures key generalizations about these forms such as the fact that a verb always takes *-en/ed* when it is preceded by *have*, or *-ing* when it is preceded by *be*.

8.3   Summary and Consequences

In conclusion, the AH analysis is better, for the reasons just stated, but if correct, this analysis has some large consequences for the theory. What sort of a rule is AH? It isn't a PS rule. PS rules only state the mother–daughter–sister relations among constituents. AH is instead a structure-changing rule – it takes a structure such as (13) as input and gives a different structure such as (14) as output. Such rules are called **transformational rules**, or simply **transformations**. If the AH analysis is on the right track, this means that sentences may have an initial structure that is "abstract" – that is, it doesn't look like English at first. Then rules like AH transform the structure into its English-like (or whatever the language is) final appearance. The term for the initial "abstract" structure is **deep structure** or **D-str**, and the term for its final form is **surface structure** or **S-str**. The AH rule that we have seen here was an early "classic" transformational rule, and there has since been much debate on whether it should be maintained. Nonetheless, we'll use it here as a heuristic to develop other ideas of transformational analysis. As a final note, there are theories of syntax that argue that transformations are unnecessary. The matter is far from settled – here we'll explore the transformational track of syntactic analysis.

Summary Points of This Chapter

- Auxiliary verbs and main verbs form **verb sequences**.
- Omissibility data (VP deletion) point toward a **recursive VP analysis** of auxiliary verbs as being the superior analysis.
- If auxiliary verbs are entered in the lexicon as **complex items** consisting of the verb and the affix that it requires the following verb to bear, then a rule of **Affix Hopping** can explain the surface distribution of affixes in a general way.
- A rule such as Affix Hopping is not a PS rule, but a **transformational rule**, one that effects a change in a syntactic structure.
- Given the presence of transformational rules in the grammar, sentence formation may involve multiple stages, with transformational rules producing the **surface structure** form of the sentence.

- The presence of transformational rules in the grammatical system opens the possibility that the initial structure of a sentence, the **deep structure** form, as formed by the PS rules, is abstract in that it does not look like a normal sentence of the language.
- The possible presence of rules that produce non-surface-like structures sheds further doubt on the idea that children acquire the grammar of a language by simply observing the surface forms that they are exposed to.

Problems

1. Use the recursive VP/Affix Hopping analysis to draw the D-str tree for each sentence below. Then show how Affix Hopping applies to derive the surface form.
   a. Mary might be telling Max a story about ducks.
   b. Flying saucers have arrived in the city park.
   c. They could have been swimming.
   d. We will play chess.
   e. Mary was driving a hotrod.
   f. They had sold the last ticket.
   g. Max has believed that Mary is mowing his lawn.

swim, V, . . .,	Args:	Cats:	Theta roles:
	1	NP	agent
	(2	NP	theme)

2. Write a brief essay recapping the argument for the "recursive VP" analysis of auxiliary verbs as follows:
   a. State the problem – how to explain the sequence of auxiliary and main verbs that may occur in simple English sentences.
   b. Spell out the two hypotheses.
   c. Spell out the VP deletion facts.
   d. Say how each hypothesis succeeds or fails to describe/predict the VP deletion facts.
   e. Conclude, based on the results in part (d), which hypothesis is better.

3. (**Advanced**) Coordination provides further evidence for the recursive VP analysis of auxiliary verbs. Consider the following sentences.
   i. Mary has been mowing the lawn and watering the flowers.
   ii. Mary has been mowing the lawn and been watering the flowers.

iii. Mary has been mowing the lawn and has been watering the flowers.

a. Continuing to assume that only phrases or single words may be coordinated, draw the deep structure tree for each of the three sentences above according to the Recursive VP hypothesis.
b. Show how Affix Hopping would operate to bring each structure to its surface structure form.
c. Under the same assumptions about coordination as above, which of the above sentences could be assigned a tree under the Complex Aux hypothesis, and which could not?
d. For any that could not be assigned a tree, explain why.
e. Given that the above sentences are all grammatical, which analysis makes the better predictions about possible grammatical sentences, and is therefore preferable?

9

Real vs. Apparent Sentence Structure

As we saw in the last chapter, there is reason to think that syntactic structures might not start out looking as they do on the surface. The theory of syntax that we are now confronted with looks like this. For a given sentence, the PS rules and the lexicon together produce an "abstract" structure that we have referred to as **deep structure** or **D-str**. This structure is then acted upon by structure-changing rules or **transformations**, which are responsible for creating the **surface structure** or **S-str** for the sentence. By the term "abstract" used above, I mean that an initial/starting sentence structure may be quite different from the surface form of the sentence. In this chapter, we'll consider phenomena that point toward a significant degree of abstractness of structure. The more abstract the structures are, the deeper the mystery is of how children acquire language – how do children acquire structures that are not surface-like?

One of the big breakthroughs in linguistic theory was the discovery by Chomsky (1957 and later) that tense affixes (the simple present tense -*s* and the simple past tense -*ed* on verbs, including their variant forms, as discussed earlier in Chapter 2) behave in certain crucial respects like independent (modal) auxiliary verbs rather than like affixes – a really surprising result. Here is some evidence for this idea.

9.1   Yes/No Questions and Tense

Yes/no questions (YNQs) are questions whose ideal answer is simply "yes" or "no." Consider the data in (1) concerning how YNQs are formed in English:

Syntactic Analysis: *The Basics*   Nicholas Sobin
© 2011 Nicholas Sobin

(1) a. Mary will walk Fido.   ⇒   Will Mary _ walk Fido?
    b. Mary is walking Fido.   ⇒   Is Mary _ walking Fido?
    c. Mary could have
       walked Fido.   ⇒   Could Mary _ have walked Fido?

Just looking at these surface forms, if we assume that questions are formed from statement-like structures, we might say that YNQs are formed according to the rule in (2):

(2) **Subject–Auxiliary Inversion(SAI)**
    YNQs are formed by moving the first post-subject auxiliary (= [+ Aux]) verb to pre-subject position.

This rule is often called "Subject–Auxiliary Inversion" because that's what it does – it inverts the subject and the first auxiliary verb. Since the moved verb has to be a part of the tree, let's temporarily assume that this moved verb adjoins leftward to S. Let's further assume that M(odal) verbs have the feature [+ Aux] just as *have* and *be* do. Thus, rule (2) will transform structure (3) into structure (4).

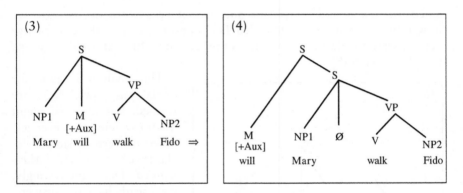

All of the YNQs in (1) would be produced in this way. In (1b), rule (2) would move the [+ Aux] verb *is*, and in (1c), it would move the [+ Aux] modal verb *could*.

This way of forming YNQs looks completely general, except for one surprising exceptional structure: sentences with no auxiliary verb. Consider the sentences in (5):

(5) Mary walked Fido.   =?⇒   Did Mary walk Fido?

The generalization appears to break down here – it appears that the simplest YNQs are formed by some different rule or process, not a compelling conclusion from a scientific standpoint (loss of generality)! So, as scientists trying to solve this puzzle, let's pose this question: What would the structure of the sentence have to look like in order to allow uniform YNQ formation by SAI (the otherwise "universal" strategy for forming English YNQs), that is, to allow rule (2) to produce all YNQs, including the one in (5)?

Consider the possibility that the tense affixes are not starting off on verbs but instead are originating in the M position, as in (6). Then, SAI would produce (7).

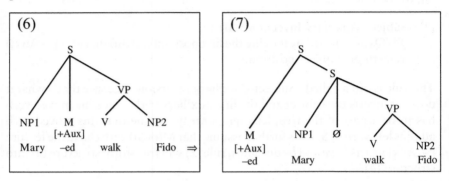

Since *-ed* is a bound morpheme and cannot be a word on its own, we now need an additional rule called *Do*-Support, which adds an expletive verb (a semantic dummy) *do* to the stranded tense affix *-ed*, yielding *do -ed* (= "did"), as in (8).

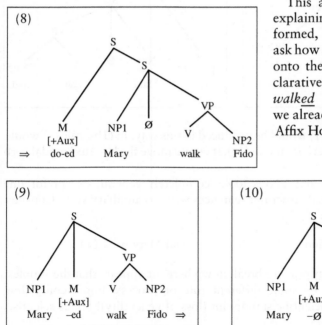

This analysis is good for explaining how YNQs are formed, but now we might ask how a tense affix ever gets onto the verb in simple declarative sentences like *Mary walked Fido*. Interestingly, we already have the answer – Affix Hopping, as in (9–10).

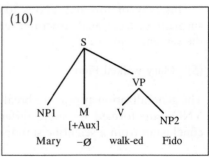

When a proposed rule such as AH proves even more useful than we originally thought in explaining additional facts (that is, its work is "automatically" expanded), that is evidence that the rule is on the right track, that the generalization that the rule embodies is even more significant.

At this point, we might wonder why the moved *-ed* in (7) would not affix-hop onto the verb? In order for an affix to affix hop, the verb must be to its immediate right. Since the verb does not immediately follow *-ed* in (7), *Do-Support* is the only alternative.

If tense affixes are inherently M-type elements, then D-str is indeed abstract – very different from S-str. Actually, in more recent analyses, the "M" position has been renamed the "T(ense)" position for the fact that the tense affixes appear there. We will follow this notational change from this point on. Now tense affixes and modal verbs will be classified as "T-type elements," and the rule creating the top structure of sentences would look like (11):

(11)   S → NP   T   VP

9.2   Negation

Negation, or more succinctly, how the negative element *not* is positioned in negative sentences, offers more evidence for the claim that tense affixes, like modal verbs, are independent T-type elements at D-str. Just considering surface sequencing for the moment, notice the relative position of *not* in the negative sentences of (12):

(12)   a. Mary will walk Fido.   ⇒   Mary will *not* walk Fido.
       b. Mary is walking Fido.   ⇒   Mary is *not* walking Fido.
       c. Mary could have walked Fido. ⇒   Mary could *not* have
                                            walked Fido.

Here it appears that *not* is normally positioned after the first auxiliary (= [+Aux]) verb.

Now consider how really simple sentences such as (13) position the negative element *not*:

(13)   Mary walked Fido.   =?⇒   Mary did not walk Fido.

Here again we seem to have a surface inconsistency as we did with YNQs – the formation of negative sentences as in (13) appears on the surface to be very different from the formation of most other negative sentences, as illustrated in (12). However, our hypothesis that tense affixes position like modal verbs comes to the rescue. If the D-str alignment of elements is as in (14), then *not* in negative sentences like (13) is being positioned after the first auxiliary element exactly as in other negative constructions.

(14)   Mary   -ed   walk Fido ⇒ Mary   -ed   not walk Fido
           [+Aux]   [+Aux]

Notice that the tense affix in the negative sentence is "stranded" – separated from the verb, but we already have a mechanism to rescue it – *Do*-Support, which would produce sentence (15):

(15)   Mary   do -ed   not   walk   Fido
           [+Aux]

So the system that we have devised automatically explains why sentences like (13) with a simple tense affix and no other auxiliary verb have a negative form with *do*. That this theory of syntax explains the syntax of negation so elegantly is further evidence that it is on the right track.

9.3   V-to-T Movement

When we consider more closely how to integrate the positioning of *not* into the system of rules, a problem becomes apparent. Rule set (16) represents a partial set of revised PS rules that account for negative placement. These rules also position VP differently, as we shall see.

(16)   **PS rules and lexicon including T and Neg**

S	→	NP	TP
TP	→	T	NegP/VP
NegP	→	Neg	VP
VP	→	V [+Aux]	VP
VP	→	V (NP)	({NP/AjP/PP})
PP	→	P	NP
NP	→	(D) (AjP)	N
AjP	→	(Int)	Aj

Here, S has only two daughters, NP and TP (Tense Phrase). TP has a head T and either NegP (Negative Phrase) or VP as a complement. NegP will introduce Neg (*not*) and VP. The rest is as we've seen before. Some sample trees are given in (17–21).

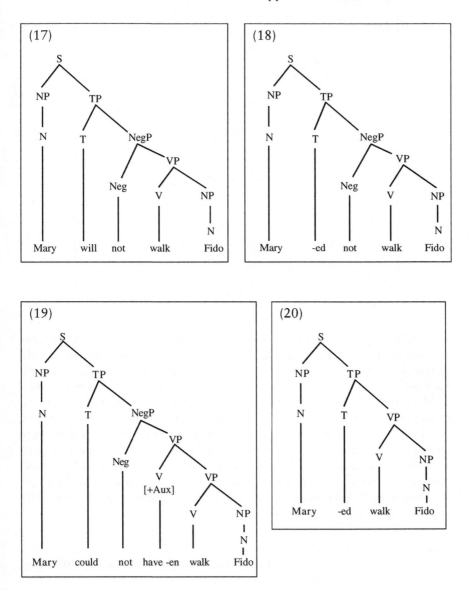

The D-strs (17) through (20) will produce the correct surface forms. In (17), everything is as it should be from the start. In (18), Do-Support will produce *Mary did not walk Fido*. In (19), AH will hop the affix *-en* onto *walk*, giving its past participle form *walked*, resulting in the sentence *Mary could not have walked Fido*. In (20), AH hops *-ed* onto *walk*, giving

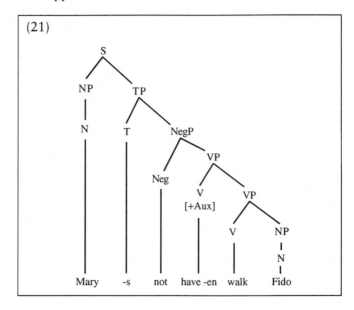

Mary walked Fido. Structure (21) presents the only problem. Here, the tense appears to be stranded – separated from any verb – so *Do*-Support should kick in. But it doesn't – we don't see *do* in such sentences (e.g. **Mary does not have walked Fido*). Instead, we somehow have to get *Mary has not walked Fido*. Notice that auxiliary verbs like *have* appear to the right of *not* when a modal verb is present, as in (19), but when T is only a tense affix as in (21), auxiliary verbs like *have* appear to the left of *not*, as though they were modal verbs positioned in T. Therefore, we might take this as evidence of another rule at work, one that moves *have* or *be* from its initial V[+Aux] position to the T position when T contains only a tense affix. This rule is called **V-to-T Movement** (or simply V-to-T), and it is given informally in (22):

(22)   **V-to-T Movement**
       If T contains only an affix, then move an immediately following V[+Aux] base to T.

A couple of things are important to note here. First, this rule moves only auxiliary verbs and not main verbs (though it actually does move main verbs in certain languages other than English). Second, recall that the English auxiliary verbs are complex lexical entries consisting of a verb base and an affix (e.g. [have -en]). This rule raises only the verb base to T, leaving the affix behind. The affix subsequently undergoes AH onto the verb to its right.

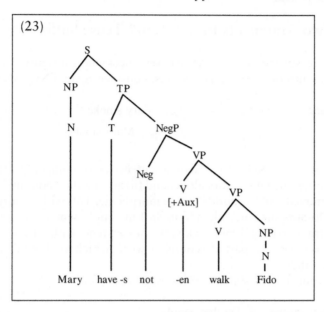

So, starting with the D-str (21), V-to-T would give (23), and AH would give (24). V-toT applies any time that (i) T contains only a tense affix and (ii) there is an auxiliary verb present in the structure, whether the sentence is negative or not.

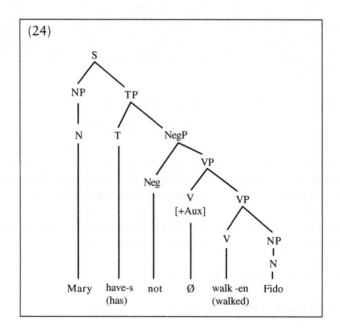

9.4   Two Arguments for a "Zero" Tense Suffix

There are reasons to think that even in sentences where no tense affix is visible, one is present nonetheless. To see this, consider again YNQs such as (25):

(25)   Mary -s_{pres} smoke $\Rightarrow$ -s_{pres} Mary smoke _

$\Rightarrow$ do -s_{pres} Mary smoke _ ?

As we've seen, a YNQ is formed on a sentence containing only a simple verb by (i) fronting the tense suffix alone, and (ii) adding the "dummy" verb *do* to the now moved and "stranded" tense morpheme. The evident purpose of the rule of *Do*-Support (the rule adding *do*) in simple sentences like (25) is to allow a stranded bound morpheme, the moved tense suffix, to be attached to a verb so as to become part of a complete word, which its "bound morpheme" status demands.

Now, consider the statement/question set in (26):

(26)   They smoke $\Rightarrow$ Do they smoke?

At first the presence of *do* looks mysterious since there is no tense affix on the surface. However, we can easily explain why the question form here requires *do* if we recognize a "zero" present tense affix -$\emptyset_{pres}$ as being present in the structure. This "zero" present tense affix is just as real as the other tense affixes such as -s_{pres}. As in (25) above, the -$\emptyset_{pres}$ affix is moved to form the question, it consequently gets "stranded," and it must be "saved" by *Do*-Support. Thus we get the question form with *do*. This is shown in (27):

(27)   They   smoke -$\emptyset_{pres}$ $\Rightarrow$ -$\emptyset_{pres}$ they smoke _

$\Rightarrow$ Do -$\emptyset_{pres}$ they smoke _ ?

The alternative is to say that *do* appears in (26) for completely different reasons than it does in (25), not an appealing alternative because it would attribute the presence of *do* to different causes rather than giving it a single, unified explanation.

Further evidence for the presence of such zero affixes involves considerations of meaning. Consider sentences (28) and (29):

(28)   She smokes. (She smoke -s_{pres})

(29)   She smoked. (She smoke -d_{pst})

Recalling the discussion in Chapter 2, the temporal information that (28) is "present" and (29) is "past" comes in part from the suffixes here, and not from the verb stem "smoke." Consider next sentences (30) and (31):

(30)   They smoke.

(31)   They smoked.

(31) shows the past tense suffix, the source for the "past" meaning. (30) shows no suffix on the surface, but the meaning "present" is here just as strongly as it is in (28). How is this to be explained if, as claimed above, the stem *smoke* does not convey temporal information? The paradox is resolved if we say that there is a "zero" present tense affix $-\emptyset_{pres}$. It is just as real as $-s_{pres}$ and is responsible for the "present" interpretation of (30). That is, (30) really has the elements shown in (32):

(32)   They smoke $-\emptyset_{pres}$

Attributing the "present" meaning of (30) to something else (claiming that the meaning "present" has multiple sources) is less desirable – it would entail a loss of generality.

9.5   A Summary of the System of Syntax

Below is a summary of the system as we have developed it thus far. It will undergo further changes (that's the nature of theory building), but it is worth trying to do derivations with this rule system to ensure understanding of how it works and what it projects as regards possible and impossible sentences.

Phrase Structure Rules:

S	→	NP	TP
TP	→	T	NegP/VP
NegP	→	Neg	VP
VP	→	V [+Aux]	VP
VP	→	V	(NP) ({NP/AjP/PP})
PP	→	P	NP
NP	→	(D)	(AjP) N
AjP	→	(Int)	Aj
NP	→	Comp	S
NP	→	NP	PP
VP	→	VP	PP
X	→	X	Conj X
XP	→	ProXP	

Some key lexical information:

T   →   [-s$_{pres}$]/[-ed$_{past}$]/[-Ø$_{pres}$]
                                (These are tense affixes.)

T   →   [can]/[could]/[will]/[would]/[may]/etc.

T   →   [to]

V$_{[+Aux]}$ →   [have -en]/[be -ing]/[be -en]

(NB: -s$_{pres}$, -ed$_{pst}$, -Ø$_{pres}$, -en, and -ing are [+ affix].)

GF interpretation and argument structure satisfaction:
GF interpretation and argument structure requirements are met/satisfied at D-str.

Some transformations and other devices (stated informally):

V-to-T:
If T is only an affix, then move an immediately following V[+ Aux] base to T, and attach the affix to it.

        (e.g., [$_T$-s]   [$_V$ have -en] becomes [$_T$ have-s]   [$_V$ Ø -en].)

Subject–Aux Inversion: (Found in questions)
Move T to pre-S position and adjoin it to S.

        (e.g. [$_{S0}$ NP   T ...]   ⇒   [$_{S1}$ T [$_{S0}$ NP   Ø ...]])

Affix Hopping:
"Hop" an affix onto the verb to its immediate right.

        (e.g. [+ affix]   V   ⇒   Ø   V + [+ affix])

***Do*-Support:**
Attach *do* to a stranded tense affix, that is, to a tense affix that is not to the immediate right of a V and cannot "affix hop" onto it.

Summary Points of This Chapter

- There is further evidence that the grammatical system of a language involves PS rules that produce the **deep structure** of a given sentence and **transformational rules** that operate on such structures and alter them, resulting in the **surface structure** form of sentences.
- The deep structure produced by the PS rules is **abstract** in the sense that it does not look like the surface form that the sentence will eventually assume.
- The **tense affixes** -*s* and -*ed* are positioned in deep structure like modal verbs. Their pre-subject surface positioning in **yes/no questions** is due to a general transformational rule of **Subject–Auxiliary Inversion**. The expletive verb *do* appears whenever a tense affix becomes stranded via a rule of *Do*-**Support**.
- The tense affixes in **declarative sentences** appear on main verbs due to **Affix Hopping**. The fact that this rule, which is already needed elsewhere, can "automatically" explain the positioning of tense affixes on verbs constitutes further evidence for viability of this rule and for the analysis in general.
- The same system of rules with the addition of the transformation **V-to-T** correctly predicts the positioning of tense affixes, the occurrence of *do*, and the positioning of *have* and *be* in negative sentences. All of this offers further support for the correctness of this approach.

Problems

1. Using the grammar developed in this chapter, for each sentence below, draw a detailed D-str, and note (in words) what each transformational rule does to the particular sentence under consideration in its derivation to S-str.

    a. Mary likes bagels.
    b. Jane might have been visiting Berlin.
    c. Did the girl win the prize?
    d. Will the girl win the prize?
    e. Is the girl winning the race?
    f. Has anyone been watching that show?
    g. Mary does not like the bagels.
    h. Mary is not taking the train.

like, V, …,	Args:	Cats:	Theta roles:
	1	NP	experiencer
	2	NP	theme
visit, V, …,	Args:	Cats:	Theta roles:
	1	NP	agent
	2	NP	theme
win, V, …,	Args:	Cats:	Theta roles:
	1	NP	experiencer
	2	NP	theme
watch, V, …,	Args:	Cats:	Theta roles:
	1	NP	agent
	2	NP	theme
take, V, …,	Args:	Cats:	Theta roles:
	1	NP	agent
	2	NP	theme

2. Recap one of the arguments for the presence of a "zero" present tense affix in such sentences as *We eat spam*.

3. (**Advanced**) Consider the following German sentences.

   i. Max hat   ein   Schiff gesehen.
     Max has   a   ship   seen
     'Max saw   a   ship.'

  ii. Max wird ein   Schiff sehen.
     Max will   a   ship see
     'Max will see a ship.'

  iii. Hat Max ein   Schiff gesehen?
     has Max a   ship   seen
     'Did Max see a ship?'

  iv. Wird Max ein   Schiff sehen?
     will Max a   ship see
     'Will Max see a ship?'

  v. Sieht Max ein   Schiff?
     sees Max a   ship
     'Does Max see a ship?'

The German root for the verb *see is seh-*. The form *ge-seh-en* is the past participle form of this verb. It utilizes the past participle circumfix (an affix that surrounds the stem that it attaches to) *ge – en*. Further, German verb roots are bound – they must appear with an affix. The affix *-en* appears on "infinitival" verbs, that is, ones that follow a modal verb, or that bear no other tense or aspectual affix.

Although the number of sentences above is few, we can begin to infer some of the syntactic properties of German. Respond to the following questions:

a. If these German sentences indicate the "deep" order of verbs and their objects, then what is the German PS rule for producing verbs with objects?

b. Are these German data compatible with an Affix Hopping analysis of affixes?

c. Assuming AH, what would the lexical entry for the equivalent of English *have* look like? (The German root is *hab-*.)

d. Considering the German VP rule above, and also assuming the recursive VP analysis of auxiliary verbs, do the German data present difficulties for the AH rule as it would operate in English? What change in the rule would be needed to make it operate correctly in German?

e. Might German have a rule of *-En*-Support (cf. *Do*-Support)? Informally, what would be the contents of this rule?

f. Do the questions in these data show evidence of Subject–Auxiliary Inversion, or of a more general verb movement rule? How might you state the rule?

10

Generalizing Syntactic Rules

Earlier we saw that some phenomena, e.g. coordination and proform insertion, appear to be category-neutral. That is, coordination and proform insertion each follow a single architecture regardless of the specific category involved, and each of these can be written as a single rule. There is evidence to suggest that perhaps the entire core system of syntax is category-neutral. In such a category-neutral system, there would not be separate rules for forming NPs, VPs, etc. Instead NPs, VPs, etc. would all follow a single architectural blue print. If this view is correct, then it represents a huge leap in the generality of the system, and that's what scientists are most interested in – capturing the rules in their most general form. We'll proceed by offering evidence that the major lexical categories all show a parallel architecture, and in the next chapter, we'll deal with the analysis of what are termed "functional" categories.

10.1 The N System

Here we'll offer some "classic" evidence for a revised, three-tiered NP structure. (Later, the development of a theory of functional categories will further impact our view of NP structure.) The PS rule that we have developed thus far for the analysis of lexically-headed NPs is the one shown in (1):

(1) NP → (D) (AjP) N

NPs with adjuncts are analyzed with rule (2):

Syntactic Analysis: *The Basics*   Nicholas Sobin
© 2011 Nicholas Sobin

(2) NP → NP PP

Now, consider NPs such as the ones in (3):

(3) a. This <u>writer of novels</u> and that <u>one</u>
    b. Mary is a <u>writer of novels</u> and <u>lover of art</u>

The rules in (1) and (2) would have us analyze the NPs containing a PP in (3) such as *this writer of novels* as shown in (4).

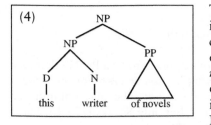

The problem with this architecture is that it can't explain the use of *one* in (3a) or the coordination in (3b). In (3a), *one* refers only to the underlined string *writer of novels*, not including the determiner. If our view of proforms as only corresponding to constituents is correct, then on the NP analysis in (4), there is no constituent to explain what *one* refers to in (3a). In (3b), the coordination does not include the determiner, as can easily be seen by reversing the coordinated elements (as in *Mary is a lover of art and writer of novels*). If, as we have been assuming, ordinary coordination requires the elements being coordinated to be either phrases or single lexical items, then the NP analysis in (4) fails to explain the possibility of the coordination seen in (3b). So, for the NPs we're dealing with here, the NP rules that we have thus far appear not to be correct.

The data in (3) seem consistently to point to an NP architecture like (5).

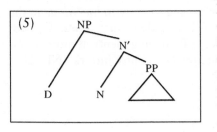

Here, the category N′ (called N-bar and originally written as N̄) unifies N and PP into a single constituent within NP, as the data in (3) seem to require. This category is what we will refer to as a "small phrase" – it is clearly phrasal and contains the lexical head – but it is not a "maximal phrase," the top N category. In (5), the maximal phrase is NP.

It is important to note immediately that the PPs in (3) are not in fact adjuncts. Consider the fact that the nouns *writer* and *lover* in (3) are related to (derived from) the verbs *write* and *love*, respectively. In verb phrases such as *writes novels* or *loves art*, the words *novels* and *art* are complements to those verbs, and they bear that same complement relationship to the nouns *writer* and *lover* in (3). So they must be differentiated as being complements and not adjuncts. With this in mind, the rules for NP might be those in (6):

(6)　a.　NP → (D) N'
　　　b.　N' → N (PP)

In rule (6b), N is the lexical head of N', and PP is its complement (sister of the head). The rules in (6) give structures like that in (5), the structure needed to explain the data in (3).

Beyond explaining the data in (3), this analysis makes further correct predictions about possible and impossible NPs. Consider the NP data in (7):

(7)　This *lover* of music with *red* hair . . .
　　　a.　. . . and that one
　　　b.　. . . and that one with *black* hair
　　　c.　. . . *and that one of *art* (with *black* hair)

As evidenced in (3) and (5), the proform *one* appears to be a ProN'; that is, it targets N' rather than NP. Now, note that in (7b), *one* refers to *lover of music*, and in (7a), *one* refers to *lover of music with red hair*. The unacceptability of (7c) shows that *one* does not simply target N, but only N', as in (7a–b). These data suggest that the structure of the NP in (7) is (8).

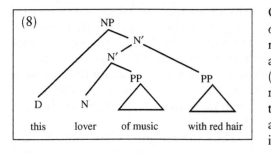

On this structural analysis, if *one* is a ProN', then it can replace/refer to the higher N', as in (7a), or the lower N', as in (7b), but not N, as the ungrammaticality of (7c) indicates. In tree (8), the PP *with red hair* is an adjunct. It clearly has nothing to do with *lover/love* in the way that *music* does. Tree (8) shows it to be structured in as an adjunct, a PP having identical mother and sister categories. If we include the adjunction possibility into the NP rules, then the NP rules are those in (9):

(9)　a.　NP → (D) N'　　(Specifier rule)
　　　b.　N' → N' PP　　(Adjunct rule)
　　　c.　N' → N (PP)　　(Complement rule)

In the NP rule (9a), the position to the left of N' is called the **specifier** or **spec** position, and that rule is called the **specifier rule**. Rule (9b) is a recursive rule introducing adjuncts at the N' level, and is called the **adjunct rule**. Rule (9c) introduces the lexical head N and any complements to N, and is called the **complement rule**. To use these rules accurately, we need to know in advance whether a given PP is or is not a complement to the particular head N involved.

Further evidence that the NP analysis in (9) is on the right track comes from other correct predictions that this analysis makes concerning other possible and impossible NPs. Since complements are only built in by rule (9c) next to the head N, a complement should always be closer to the head than an adjunct. The NPs in (10) indicate that this prediction is correct:

(10)   a. a lover of music with red hair
       b. *a lover with red hair of music

Thus, still assuming that *of music* here is a complement and *with red hair* is an adjunct, the NP rules in (9) can give a tree for (10a), namely tree (8), but not for (10b).

A second correct prediction is that adjuncts should be able to compile (as in earlier analyses) because the adjunct rule is recursive. This is verified in example (11), to which the rules in (9)would assign the structure in (12).

(11)   This lover of music with red hair by the door (with a drink ...)

(12)

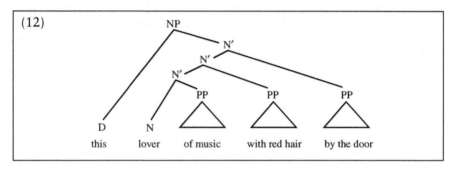

A third correct prediction is that complements will not iterate or compound, because complements are limited by the head and structured in by a non-recursive rule (9c). Thus, NPs such as (13) with multiple complements are impossible:

(13)   *a lover of music of art

10.2   The V System

Turning to verbs and verb phrases, of interest here is the discovery that VP arguably shows an architecture that parallels that of NP. To see this, consider the data in (14):

(14)   a. The girls have [$_{VP}$ each <u>bought a sports car</u>], and the boys have [$_{VP}$ each <u>done so</u>] too.
       b. The girls will [$_{VP}$ each <u>take a postcard</u> and <u>leave a quarter</u>].

Quantifiers are generally words denoting or related to quantity. In these data, we'll assume that the quantifier (Quan) *each*, though it is semantically associated with the subject, is actually situated within VP. This may seem unintuitive at first, but much more evidence will emerge later that supports this idea. However, here is one argument that *each* occurs within VP. Recall the earlier claim that auxiliary verbs such as *have* head their own VPs and take a VP complement. The fact that word sequences beginning with *each* can be coordinated below *have* as in (15) suggests that *each* in (15) is part of the innermost VP:

(15)   The girls have <u>each gotten a ticket and each paid the fine</u>.

(There are other ways to express what is said in (15), but (15) is definitely a grammatical possibility.) If *each* is indeed part of a VP, then the proform *do so* in (14a) has only a part of VP, the head and its complement, as its antecedent. Similarly in (14b), the coordinated underlined sequences consisting of verb and complement are also only a part of the VP. To explain the data in (14), we might propose that the structure of these VPs is as in (16).

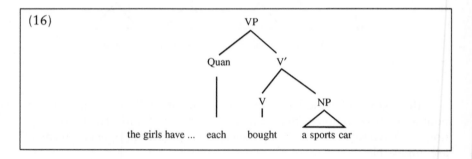

(16)

Using structure to infer what the rules ought to be, a structure for VP such as (16) would be due to rules like those in (17):

(17)   a. VP → (Quan) V'   (Specifier rule)
       b. V' → V (NP) ...   (Complement rule)

(Here, V' is called "V-bar.") These rules look quite parallel to the NP rules discussed earlier. Further, adjuncts appear also to work in parallel with NP adjuncts, as the data in (18) illustrate.

(18) The girls each lit a cigar in the living room with a match ...
    a. ... and the boys each did so too.
    b. ... and the boys each did so with a Zippo.
    c. ... and the boys each did so in the dining room with a Zippo.
    d. ... *and the boys each did so a cigarette (in the dining room) (with a Zippo).

These data may be explained in terms of a structure like (19).

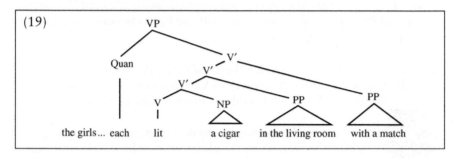

It appears that *do so* is a ProV′ (parallel to *one* as a ProN′). Then, (18a) is possible with *do so* targeting the highest V′, (18b) shows *do so* targeting the mid-level V′, and (18c) shows *do so* targeting the low V′. (18d) is bad, since *do so* targets V′ and not V, again like *one* in NPs, which targets N′ and not N. Addition of an adjunction rule fills out the rules needed for VP, as in (20):

(20) a. VP → (Quan) V′   (Specifier rule)
    b. V′ → V′ PP   (Adjunct rule)
    c. V′ → V (NP) ...   (Complement rule)

As might be expected, the same predictions about the behaviors of complements and adjuncts as held for NP also hold for VP: a complement must be closer to the head than any adjunct, as confirmed in (21a); complements are due to a recursive rule and may compile, as seen in (18) and (19) above; and complements cannot compile, as illustrated in (21b):

(21) a. *?The girls lit with a match a cigar.
    b. *The boys lit a cigar a pipe.

10.3 The Aj System and the P System

Without going into as much detail here, there is evidence to indicate that both AjPs and PPs show an architecture like the one seen in NP and

VP. For AjP, consider examples such as the one in (22), and for PP, the one in (23):

(22)   Jane is [AjP very <u>fond of Cheetah</u>], but Tarzan is [AjP less <u>so</u>].

(23)   Put the suitcase [PP over <u>by the closet</u>], and put the satchel [PP over <u>there</u>] too.

As seen in (24) and (25), the expressions *very* and *over* in (22) and (23) are part of AjP and PP respectively since, when AjP and PP are fronted, *very* and *over* move as a part of these phrases:

(24)   a. She is fond of Cheetah ⇒ Fond of Cheetah, she is __
         b. She is very fond of Cheetah ⇒ Very fond of Cheetah, she is __
         c. She is very fond of Cheetah ⇒ *Fond of Cheetah, she is very __

(25)   a. I put the suitcase by the closet ⇒ By the closet, I put the suitcase __
         b. I put the suitcase over by the closet ⇒ Over by the closet, I put the suitcase __
         c. I put the suitcase over by the closet ⇒ *By the closet, I put the suitcase over __

   Now, given that *very* and *over* are part of AjP and PP respectively, what we see in (22) and (23) is once again a proform targeting only the head-and-complement portion of these phrases. The architecture that these data point to is seen in (26) and (27).

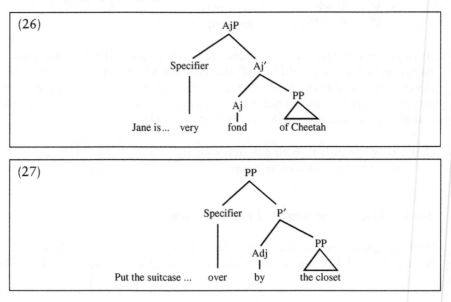

10.4   Category-Neutral Rules

In sum, all of the major categories that we have considered (NP, VP, AjP, and PP) appear to share the same basic architecture, the one illustrated in (28).

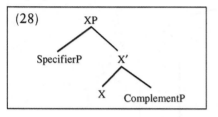

(28)

In (28), X is any lexical head. X and the ComplementP(hrase) form a small phrase, X'. X' combines with SpecifierP(hrase) to form the maximal phrase, XP. The generalized rules, allowing for adjuncts as we have above, are given in (29):

(29) a. XP → (SpecifierP) X'
      b. X' → X' AdjunctP
      c. X' → X (ComplementP)

As we shall see, there is much evidence that the Spec position is actually a phrasal one, like the complement and adjunct positions. Of course, Xs don't appear in trees. Let's say that we have a verb like *wash* with its lexical entry as in (30) (See chapter 5):

(30) *wash*, V,..., | Args: | Cats: | Theta roles:
      | | 1 | NP | agent
      | | 2 | NP | theme

This verb must head a VP, whose complement will be an NP, and whose subject will also be an NP. So the tree for such a sentence will have these categories in it, as dictated by the verb. We won't attempt the tree yet, because the next chapter, which deals with the extension of X-bar syntax to all categories, will have a large impact on how sentences are analyzed. But a partial tree following the rules in (29) and showing the VP portion of the sentence *The girls each washed a motorcycle right by the garage* (where the adjunct means where this happened), is shown in (31).

The parentheses surrounding specifiers and complements in the rules of (29) indicate that each may be present or absent. Thus, these rules allow correctly for phrases either with or without complements (e.g. *a player of the violin* and *a player*) and with or without specifiers (e.g. *a lover of music* and *lovers of music*). Interestingly, the possibility that a complement might or might not be present in conjunction with the preceding X-bar analysis of phrasal structure explains the surprising fact that sometimes a given word can be the antecedent of a proform and at other

(31)

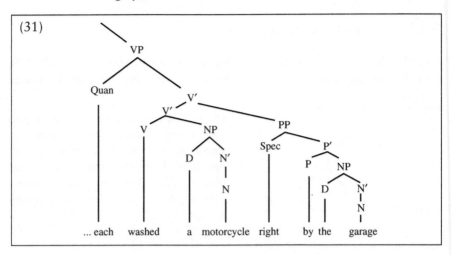

times it cannot be. For example, *player* can be targeted by *one* in (32a) but not in (32b).

(32)   a. This <u>player</u> and that <u>one</u>
       b. *This <u>player</u> of the violin and that <u>one</u> of the piano

This is because *this player* in (32a) would have the structure in (33a), where *player* is the sole content of an N′. Since *one* is a ProN′, it can use the N′ *player* as an antecedent.

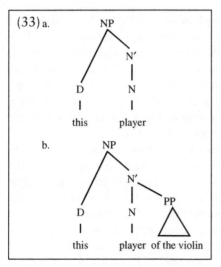

In contrast, *player* in (32b/33b) is only an N and not an N′, and so it cannot be an antecedent for the ProN′ *one*. The parallel facts can be seen in the V system with *do so* and verbs. Some verbs such as *eat* may or may not display a complement. As seen in (34/35), when no complement is present, *do so* appears to use the verb as an antecedent, due to the fact that it is the sole content of a V′. When a complement is present, the verb is not the sole content of a V′, and cannot be targeted by *do so*.

(34)   a. The girls (each) <u>ate</u>, and the boys (each) <u>did so</u> too.
      b. *The girls (each) <u>ate</u> a hamburger, and the boys (each) <u>did so</u> a
        cheeseburger.

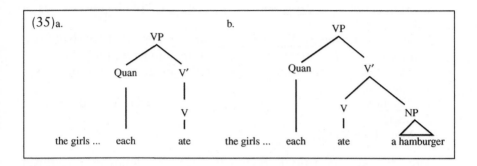

The ability of this theory to deal successfully with such additional and otherwise hard-to-explain facts is strong evidence for its correctness relative to the structural theories that were being considered earlier. That does not mean that this theory is ultimately correct, but that it is the best one considered so far. That is the nature of scientific inquiry.

Summary Points of This Chapter

- The earlier hypotheses about the structure of the major categories NP, VP, etc. cannot explain the use of proforms such as *one* and *do so*, or certain coordination possibilities.
- The major categories appear to have a three-level structure involving **small phrases** that include only the head and complement(s) of a phrase.
- **Maximal phrases** immediately consist of a small phrase and a possible **specifier**.
- **Adjunct phrases** are adjoined to small phrases.
- The major lexical categories all appear to share a common **category-neutral** architecture.
- Following the norms of gauging success in scientific inquiry, the category-neutral theory is preferable to the earlier category-specific theory due to its success in explaining data that the earlier theory could not explain, and its greater economy and generality, the normal indicators of the "correctness" of a given theory.

Problems

1. Draw the category-neutral structure for each of the following underlined NPs:

   a. Max visited <u>a professor of linguistics</u>. ("of linguistics" is a complement)
   b. We saw <u>a game of baseball with extra innings</u> ("of baseball" is a complement and "with extra innings" is an adjunct within NP)
   c. The students each sang <u>a verse of the song</u>. ("of the song" is a complement)
   d. <u>The box over by the door</u> belongs to Mary ("over by the door" is an adjunct)
   e. Mary likes <u>spinach</u>.

2. Draw the category-neutral structure for each of the following underlined VPs:

   a. Mary <u>plays the piano</u>.
   b. Mary <u>left the party in a huff</u>.
   c. Mary <u>sold a guitar to Max for $20</u>.
   d. Mary <u>smiled despite the weather</u>.
   e. Mary <u>put the plates on the table</u>.

3. Draw the category-neutral structure for each of the following underlined AjPs and PPs:

   a. Jane is <u>fond of Cheetah</u>.
   b. She is <u>very proud of Tarzan</u>.
   c. She is <u>angry at the outcome of the game</u>.
   d. She was <u>very angry</u>.
   e. Mary stood <u>right by the door</u>.

4. Write a brief essay recapping one of the arguments (either *one* pronominalization or phrase-internal coordination) for the N/N′/NP (X-bar) analysis of NP as follows:

   a. Show the relevant data.
   b. Explain the difficulty that the earlier N/NP theory encounters with these data.
   c. Spell out the N/N′/NP theory.
   d. Explain how the N/N′/NP theory can deal with the same facts.
   e. Conclude, based on a comparison of the success of each theory in dealing with the facts, which theory is better.

5. Recap the argument that *each* in a sentence like *The girls have each spent a dollar* occupies a Specifier-of-VP position.

6. (**Advanced**) In this theory, auxiliary verbs head VPs, which would also have X-bar structure. Assuming that *each* likes to occupy some Specifier-of-VP position, draw the structure of each of the following underlined VP structures:

   a. The girls <u>have each been visiting the zoo</u>.
   b. The girls <u>each have been visiting the zoo</u>.

7. (**Advanced**) Assuming X-bar syntax, what would be the two trees which would explain the structural ambiguity of the sentence *Mary painted the cabinet in the garage*?

8. (**Advanced**) The complements and adjuncts in NPs not only appear in post-nominal position (as in *a lover of music with red hair*), but also in prenominal position, as in *a tall music lover* or *a red-haired music lover*. That an expression like *tall* (or *red-haired*) is an adjunct and *music* is a complement can be seen by considering the following data:

   i. a tall music lover and a short one   (one = music lover)
   ii. this tall music lover and that one   (one = tall music lover)
   iii. *a tall music lover and a short art one
   iv. *a music tall lover
   v. a tall, smart music lover
   vi. *a music art lover

Discuss how these data point toward the conclusion that *music* (and also *art*) is a complement, whereas *tall* (and also *smart* and *short*) is an adjunct.

11

Functional Categories

The **functional category hypothesis (FCH)** is the hypothesis that functional categories such as T(ense) and C(omplementizer) are not only present in syntactic structure but also play key roles in how sentences are structured and in how and why derivational processes such as the movement of constituents from one position in a sentence to another take place. Here, we'll consider evidence pointing toward the possibility that **functional categories** are structured into sentences following the same category-neutral architecture that we have posited for NP, VP, AjP, and PP. If indeed they can be demonstrated to be in compliance with X-bar architecture, then the system of category-neutral syntax would appear to be even more general. Let's first consider arguments that C projects an X-bar structure.

11.1   C as an X-bar Category

Consider the following four observations. At first, they may appear somewhat diverse and unrelated. However, they all come together in positing an X-bar analysis of C.

First, the data in (1) offer evidence that C and S form a constituent.

(1)   a.   I believe [that$_C$ [$_S$ Mary likes fishing]] and [that$_C$ [$_S$ Jane prefers jogging]].
   b.   Speaker A: I believe [that Mary likes fishing]; Speaker B: I don't believe <u>it</u>.

In (1a) we see C (=<u>that</u>) and S together forming each of the elements of a coordination. If coordinatability indicates phrasehood, as we have

Syntactic Analysis: *The Basics*   Nicholas Sobin
© 2011 Nicholas Sobin

established, then C and S together form a phrase. Similarly in (1b), C and S together form the antecedent of the proform *it*. Following our analysis of proforms as only having phrasal antecedents, this also points toward the conclusion that C and S form a phrase.

Second, auxiliary verbs (including modal verbs) in embedded YNQs seem to be in active competition with interrogative C (= *whether/if*) for the C position. This is seen in the data of (2):

(2)   a. They asked [whether [Mary will be here]]
      b. They asked [will [Mary _ be here]]
      c. *They asked [whether will [Mary _ be here]]

As seen in (2a), an embedded question may be preceded by the interrogative C (here, *whether*). Alternatively, many English speakers move an auxiliary verb such as the T-positioned modal verb *will* to pre-subject position, as in (2b). That is, T appears to be moving to the C position. The impossibility of (2c) suggests further that both are competing for the same single pre-subject position (the C position) since only one or the other may appear, but not both.

Third, as the data in (3) show, root YNQs show the same movement of an auxiliary verb in T to pre-subject position as seen above in embedded questions such as (2b). If the movement in (2b) is T-to-C, then the same movement in root clauses points toward the conclusion that root clauses also have a C position.

(3)   [Will [Mary _ be here]]?

Fourth, in root *wh* questions (WHQs – ones involving a *wh* phrase such as *what*, *who*, or *how*) the *wh* phrase moves left **past the C position** (which is occupied by the moved auxiliary verb), as illustrated in (4):

(4)   [What can [Mary _ see _]]?

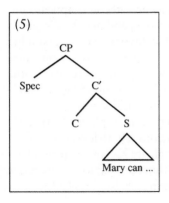

(5)

All of these seemingly disparate facts can be made sense of by analyzing C as having an X-bar architecture. In this proposal, both embedded and root sentences are housed in a complementizer Phrase (CP), as in (5).

This architecture provides us with an interesting basis for explaining the various facts we have just been considering. First, if C is an X-bar category as in (5), then C and S necessarily form a constituent, namely, C′ (and CP, if no specifier is present). Second, the C position explains not only where complementizers appear, when they do appear, but, it also provides a possible "landing site" for a moved auxiliary verb when C is phonetically "empty" (that is, not filled with a phonetically realized complementizer). This sort of movement of a head to the nearest c-commanding head position is quite similar to the rule of V-to-T movement argued for earlier in Chapter 9. The movement of an auxiliary verb from T to C is another instance of this general type of movement, which is called **head movement**. As seen in (2) and (3), such movement may (must) take place in embedded questions when C is phonetically empty (e.g. no one says *I wonder Mary will be here*), and it must take place in root questions, where interrogative C (in English) is always phonetically empty (e.g. no one says *Whether Mary will be here?* meaning "will Mary be here?"). Finally, X-bar architecture projects a Spec position for CP, and this appears to provide the landing site for moved *wh*-phrases in WHQs. So it appears that X-bar architecture offers an account of all of the preceding data involving C.

11.2   The X-bar Treatment of T and S

Next, what about T? As we've already seen, T (which may contain a modal auxiliary verb or a tense affix) is independent of V in the "deep" syntax. If we simply assume that T should have X-bar architecture, then we get the structure in (6), which turns out to be very useful.

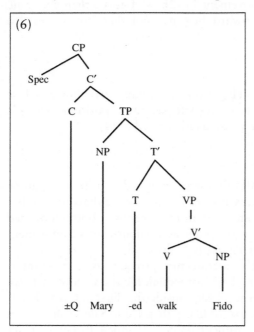

(6)

Here, T combines with VP to form T′. The X-bar hypothesis predicts a possible Spec position for TP, and that would be the position in which subjects appear. Given this result, then S, which does not comply with X-bar architecture, appears unnecessary, and may be dispensed with in favor of TP. So, assuming that T has X-bar architecture "automatically" resolves the questions surrounding the possible structural status of S.

Thus, it is plausible that all categories, both lexical and functional, are X-bar categories. Further, considering structures such as (6), it appears that the functional categories may provide the "basic skeletal structure" for sentences (= the FCH).

A few more observations about these ideas are in order. Just as T encodes a core piece of **temporal** information, information relevant to when the proposition encoded by the sentence is being said to hold or take place, so C encodes the "force" of the clause, information about whether the clause is **declarative** (a statement) or **interrogative** (a question). This is clearly illustrated in the case of embedded sentences, where the complementizer *that* is used if the embedded clause is a statement, as in (7a), and the complementizer *whether* or *if* is used if the embedded clause is a question, as in (7b):

(7) a. I believe that Mary will like oysters.
     (= *I believe something: Mary will like oysters.*)

     b. I wonder whether Mary will like oysters.
     (= *I wonder something: Will Mary like oysters?*)

In the case of declaratives, the C position may be empty, so we can also have (8) as another version of (7a):

(8) I believe Mary will like the oysters.

Notice, however, that the embedded clause is still declarative. If the force (declarative or interrogative) of a clause is borne by/indicated by its C, then even when C is not realized phonetically, we still maintain that a declarative C is present. In (8), it is simply phonetically null, a "zero" morpheme (which we might encode as $C[-Q]$ or $\emptyset_{that}$; recall that we've already seen other instances of zero morphemes, such as the null version of present tense T in sentences such as *They want* $-\emptyset_{pres}$ *hamburgers*). The declarative C position does not require phonetic realization, so C may be lexicalized as *that* or as $\emptyset_{that}$.

In contrast to declarative C, it appears that the interrogative C position must always have some sort of phonetic realization. In embedded YNQ clauses, *whether* or *if* appears in C. If neither appears, we see an auxiliary verb moving into the C position to make it phonetic. Let's say that the interrogative C has a feature $[+Q]$ that signals that the clause it introduces is interrogative, and that forces an auxiliary verb to move from T to C to make the phonetically null C position phonetic.

Turning to root clauses, they have declarative or interrogative force just as embedded clauses do, but it appears that (in English) root clauses generally cannot display a phonetic complementizer. That's fine in the case of declaratives, which do not demand a phonetic C, as we've seen. But in the case of interrogatives, something must be done; though a root interrogative clause cannot have a lexical complementizer (*whether* or *if*), there is still the demand (seen in embedded interrogative clauses) that the interrogative C position must be phonetically realized. So the only option for a root interrogative C is the empty $C[+Q]$, which will trigger T-to-C movement, which is what we see in root YNQs. The analysis of WHQs is more complex, and that analysis will be developed later.

Returning to (6) above, if C is [+Q], then we have a question, and we should derive *Did Mary walk Fido?* If C in (6) is [−Q], then we have a statement, and we should derive *Mary walked Fido*.

11.3   Order within X-bar Architecture

As was pointed out in Problem 8 of Chapter 10, in some instances, a complement or adjunct may either precede or follow certain lexical heads. In English, a noun may have a complement and adjuncts that follow it as in (9a), that precede it, as in (9b), or that mix these positional possibilities, as in (9c) and (9d).

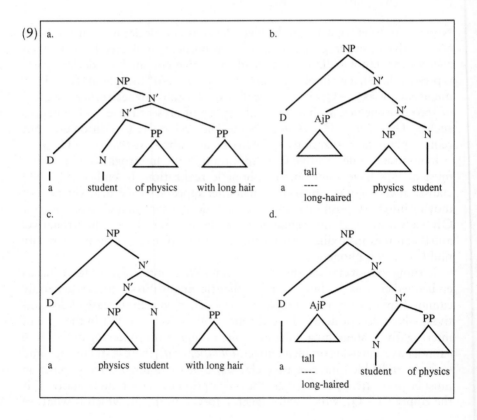

Structure (9b) shows the prenominal positioning of a single adjunct such as *tall* or *long-haired*. Prenominal adjuncts are AjPs rather than PPs, and prenominal complements are NPs rather than PPs. Structure (9c) shows a prenominal complement and a postnominal adjunct, whereas (9d) shows a prenominal adjunct and postnominal complement.

Verb phrases in English normally have postverbal complements. However, they may have post- or preverbal adjuncts. Such preverbal adjuncts are typically Adverb phrases (AvP). This is illustrated in (10).

(10)

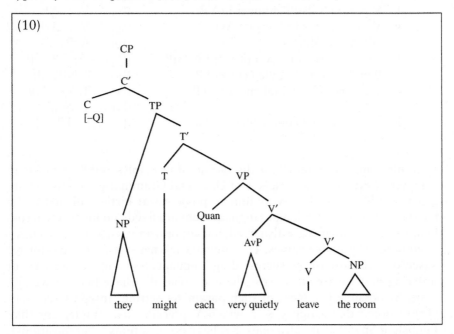

In (10), the AvP *very quietly* is a preverbal adjunct, and the NP *the room* is a postverbal complement. Structure (10) also offers an illustration of how the structure of a complete sentence including the functional categories T and C looks (minus the details of NP and AvP).

The positioning possibilities illustrated in (9) and (10) carry the implication that the very general rules that produce X-bar architecture do not strictly impose left–right order on the constituents involved. We might revise the X-bar rules as in (11), where we follow the convention that constituents separated by a comma are ones whose relative order is yet to be determined.

(11) a. XP → (SpecifierP), X′
     b. X′ → X′, AdjunctP
     c. X′ → X, (ComplementP)

A language such as English must have some additional mechanisms that result in orderings such as those described in (12):

(12) a. N precedes its PP complement in NP.   ($[_{NP} \ldots$ N PP$\ldots]$)
      b. N precedes its PP adjunct in NP.   ($[_{NP} \ldots$ N$\ldots$PP$\ldots]$)
      c. N follows its AjP adjunct in NP.   ($[_{NP} \ldots$ AjP$\ldots$N$\ldots]$)
      d. N follows its NP complement in NP.   ($[_{NP} \ldots$ NP N$\ldots]$)
      e. V precedes its complement (s) in VP.   ($[_{VP} \ldots$ V XP$\ldots]$)
      f. V precedes its PP adjunct in VP.   ($[_{VP} \ldots$ V$\ldots$PP$\ldots]$)
      g. V precedes or follows its AvP   ($[_{VP} \ldots$ V$\ldots$AvP$\ldots]$)/
          adjunct in VP.   ($[_{VP} \ldots$ AvP$\ldots$V$\ldots$)
      h. Aj precedes its PP complement in AjP.   ($[_{AjP} \ldots$ Aj PP$\ldots]$)
      i. P precedes its complement in PP.   ($[_{PP} \ldots$ P NP$\ldots]$)
      j. T precedes its complement in TP.   ($[_{TP} \ldots$ T VP$\ldots]$)/
                                                      ($[_{TP} \ldots$ T NegP$\ldots]$)
      k. C precedes its complement in CP.   ($[_{CP} \ldots$ C TP$\ldots]$)
      etc.

In this connection, recall the discussion of Principles and Parameters in Chapter 1. Principles are aspects of Universal Grammar (UG – the innate genetic endowment that every human possesses at birth, and that is the basis for learning a particular language) that are fixed and invariant across languages. Parameters are also fixed, but contain an open setting that has a fixed range of possible values. The language learner sets a given parameter based on exposure to the surrounding language. Some of the facts about ordering that we are considering here are ones that have been viewed by many as possible instances of such **parameter setting**. Joseph Greenberg (1966) noted that languages in which V precedes its complement (like English or Spanish) are also ones that have **pre**-positions (= prepositions), that is, P also precedes its complement. On the other hand, languages in which V follows its complement (such as Japanese, Quechua, or Apache) are also ones that have **post**-positions, that is, P follows its complement. Others noting Greenberg's facts proposed a parameter called the **head parameter**. This proposal says that the elements of the complement rule (namely the head and complement) are initially unordered (in UG), and the language learner must set the value of the head parameter as "head-left" or "head-right," depending on the facts of the language being learned. Thus when a language learner is exposed to a language like English where heads such as V and P are to the left of their complements, the learner sets the head parameter value as "head-left." If the learner is instead exposed to a language such as Apache with V and P following their complements, the learner sets the head parameter value as "head-right." Looking again at the list of orderings in (12), a "head-left" setting for the head parameter for English would explain in a single statement all of the orderings in (12a), (12e), (12h), (12i), (12j), and (12k). There is much more research to be done to fully understand what the parameters are and how they apply, as the apparently problematic ordering in (12d) indicates. Also, there are questions about how to explain the ordering of adjuncts. However, its success thus far in generally accounting for head–complement ordering looks very promising.

11.4   A General X-bar Syntax

The picture for the rules of syntax that emerges from the above observations and arguments is summarized below. Here, the grammar is almost entirely category-neutral.

X-bar syntax
The core architecture:

$$XP \rightarrow (YP), \ X' \quad \text{(Specifier rule)}$$
$$X' \rightarrow X', \ WP \quad \text{(Adjunct rule)}$$
$$X' \rightarrow X, \ (ZP) \quad \text{(Complement rule)}$$

Some additional rules:

$$X^n \rightarrow X^n \ Conj \ X^n \quad (X^n = any \ level \ of \ X)$$
$$XP \rightarrow ProXP$$

Some lexical information:

$$T \quad \rightarrow [\text{-s}_{pres}]/[\text{-ed}_{pst}]/[\text{-}\varnothing_{pres}] \quad \text{(These are tense affixes.)}$$
$$\rightarrow [can]/[could]/[will]/[would]/[may]/etc.$$
$$\rightarrow [to]$$
$$\underset{[+Aux]}{V} \rightarrow [have \ \text{-en}]/[be \ \text{-ing}]/[be \ \text{-en}]$$

(NB: -s_{pres}, -ed_{pst}, $\text{-}\varnothing_{pres}$, -en, and -ing are $[+affix]$.)

Argument structure: GF interpretation and Argument structure requirements must be satisfied at deep structure.

Head parameter setting: "head-left" (English)

Some transformations and other devices (stated informally):

V-to-T:
If T is only an affix, then move a following V[+ Aux] base to T, and attach the affix to it.

    (e.g., [_T_ -s] [_V_ have -en] become [_T_ have -s] [_V_ Ø -en])

T-to-C (Subject–Aux Inversion): (only in "root" questions)
Move T to C[+ Q].

$$\ldots [_C\; \varnothing\;] \; [_{TP}\;\; NP \;\; T \ldots] \;\; \Rightarrow \;\; \ldots [_C T\;] \; [_{TP}\;\; NP \;\; \varnothing \ldots])$$
$$\quad\;\; [+Q] \qquad\qquad\qquad\qquad\qquad [+Q]$$

Affix Hopping:
"Hop" an affix onto the verb to its immediate right.

    (e.g., [+ affix]   V   ⇒   Ø   V + [+ affix])

"Do"-Support:
Attach "do" to a stranded tense affix, that is, to a tense affix that is not to the immediate right of a V and cannot "affix hop" onto it.

Summary Points of This Chapter

- A variety of facts appear to support an analysis of **functional categories** as exhibiting X-bar architecture.
- Certain traditional functional categories such as S and Aux are rendered unnecessary by the treatment of T and C as X-bar categories.
- As a consequence, **X-bar** architecture (where **head** and **complement** form a **small phrase**, **adjuncts** adjoin to small phrase, and small phrase and **specifier** form a **maximal phrase**) appears to be ubiquitous in the system of syntactic structure.
- The overall result is a system of **category-neutral** syntactic architecture of much greater generality, simplicity, and explanatory value as compared to the category-specific architectures considered earlier.
- Languages vary as to how they order the elements that make up the core X-bar architecture, suggesting that the core X-bar rules specify **hierarchy**, but not **linear order** among these elements.
- The **setting** of **parameters** such as the **head parameter** may explain the consistencies of ordering across different categories of particular types of elements found in a given language.

Problems

1. The grammar in Section 4 would analyze the D-str of the sentence *Have the girls each taken a hot bagel?* as follows.

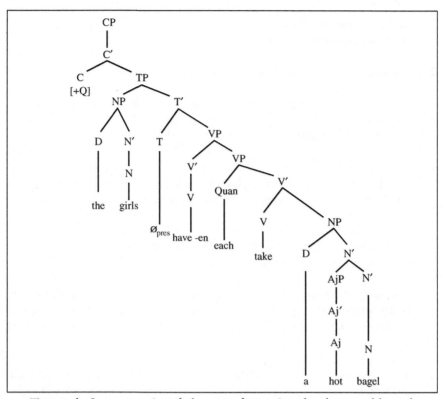

To reach S-str, certain of the transformational rules would apply as follows:

First, V-to-T moves *have* to T.
Next, T-to-C moves *have* in T (= *have* + $\emptyset_{pres}$) to C[+Q].
Finally, Affix Hopping moves *-en* onto the verb *take*.

Following the above example, draw the D-str tree for each of the following sentences, and state how each relevant transformational rule applies to derive its S-str. (As in the example, simply leave any Ds and Quans (which might appear in Spec of NP and Spec of VP, respectively) as such.)

a. Mary likes bagels.
b. Jane might have been visiting Berlin.
c. Did the girl win the prize?
d. Will the girl win the prize?
e. Is the girl winning the race?
f. Has anyone been watching that show?

g. Mary does not like the bagels.
h. Mary is not taking the train.

2. Consider the following sentences of Quechua:

i. maria uk čilwi-ta   hapʔi-sa-ŋ   koral-pi
   Maria a chick-object   catch-prog-3sg   corral-in
   'Maria is catching a chick in the corral.'

ii. maria uk pʰułu-ta   ranti-sa-ŋ   merkado-pi
    Maria a blanket-object buy-prog-3sg   market-in
    'Maria is buying a blanket in the market.'

iii. hwanito uk alpaka-ta   rikʰu-ŋ koral-pi
     Juanito an alpaca-object   see-3sg corral-in
     'Juanito sees an alpaca in the corral.'

Assuming that the surface order of verbs and their objects and postpositions (the counterpart to prepositions) and their objects is indicative of the deep order of these elements, answer the following questions:

a. Do VP and PP in Quechua show a consistent setting for the head parameter?
b. How is the head parameter set in Quechua?

3. (**Advanced**) Assuming that *each* is in the specifier of VP and that *do so* is a ProV′, use the following sentence to construct an argument that the AvP *very quietly* is a V′ adjunct:

They might have each very quietly left the room, and we could have each done so too.

12

Questions, Relative Clauses, and *WH* Movement

Here, we will extend our analysis of questions to include *WH* questions (WHQs), questions involving a *wh* phrase such as *what*, in *What can you see?* Before doing this, it is worth reflecting on relevant aspects of the grammar that we have established thus far.

12.1 Why Movement?

As we observed in the last chapter, root YNQs, and some embedded ones, are formed by moving an auxiliary verb in T to the phonetically empty inter-rogative complementizer C[+ Q]. Evidently, this complementizer requires phonetic form, which can be accomplished in embedded interrogative clauses by either choosing a phonetic complementizer (*if* or *whether*) or by T-to-C movement, as we've seen. Since a phonetic complementizer is not an option for root YNQs, these questions utilize T-to-C movement exclusively. Further, we have argued that there is a rule of V-to-T movement that moves an auxiliary verb to the T position if T is only an affix.

Let's reflect for a moment on the advantages of such movement analyses. V-to-T movement offers an easy one-rule explanation of why we see non-modal auxiliary verbs apparently vacillating in their positioning relative to *not*, as seen in (1):

(1) a. Mary would <u>not have</u> left vs. Mary <u>has not</u> left
     b. Mary would <u>not be</u> leaving vs. Mary <u>is not</u> leaving
     c. Mary might <u>not be</u> here vs. Mary <u>is not</u> here

Syntactic Analysis: *The Basics*   Nicholas Sobin
© 2011 Nicholas Sobin

T-to-C movement further offers a one-rule explanation of why in questions we see the possible post-subject verb sequence reduced from the one seen in statements by exactly the element corresponding to the question-initial verb, as illustrated in(2):

(2) a. Mary <u>has seen</u> a flying saucer ⇒ <u>Has</u> Mary _ <u>seen</u> a flying saucer?

b. She <u>could have been eating</u> some cake ⇒

<u>Could</u> she _ <u>have been eating</u> some cake?

c. She <u>is singing</u> songs ⇒ <u>Is</u> she _ <u>singing</u> songs?

Also, T-to-C movement helps to explain why the verb after the subject appears to agree with the subject in statements but not in questions. With T-to-C movement, the agreeing verb is always in the post-subject T position (the position for subject–verb agreement), and it simply moves in questions. The movement approach will prove valuable in analyzing WHQs.

12.2   Puzzles Presented by WHQs

Consider WHQs such as the ones in (3):

(3) a. What does Mary like?
    b. Where can I put the wrench?
    c. Who will want sauerkraut?
    d. Who likes sauerkraut?

These constructions pose some interesting puzzles. First, in sentences (3a) and (3b), there appear to be argument structure violations. *Like* requires an NP complement (you can't say (*Mary likes*), and *put* requires, in addition to an NP complement, a locative PP complement (you can't say *I put the wrench*). And yet, given that the *wh* phrases are clearly not positioned as complements to their respective verbs, that's exactly what we do see in (3a) and (3b) – verb phrases with apparently missing complements.

Second, we understand the *wh* phrases in (3a) and (3b) to have the requisite complement theta roles, but how are these theta roles assigned? The rules for determining grammatical functions and the consequent theta role assignments look for complements as sisters to a V or P head. Clearly, *what* and *where* in (3) are not in such positions.

Third, whereas the word order in (3a) and (3b) is very different from the word order that would be seen in corresponding declarative sentences (e.g. *Mary likes something* and *I can put the wrench there*), the word orders seen in (3c) and (3d) are exactly the same as the word orders of corresponding declarative sentences (e.g. *Someone will want sauerkraut* and *Someone likes sauerkraut*). Why do we see the apparent massive alteration of order when complements (or adjuncts) are being questioned, but not when subjects are being questioned? The following movement analysis of WHQs easily explains all of these apparent anomalies.

12.3   *WH* Movement

All of these puzzles are solved at once if we say that in WHQs, the *wh* phrases start in their "home" semantic positions at D-str (the positions required by the argument structure of the verb involved), and are moved in derivation to Spec of CP. Further, the same movements will apply to all of the sentences in (3), so that all four sentences undergo the same movement rules, despite the surface appearance that they do not, offering a **single, uniform, non-exceptional analysis** of question formation – a very desirable feature of a good theory.

Let's continue with the idea that movement of a constituent within a sentence is triggered by a feature of some item(s) within the sentence. Just as T-to-C movement is triggered by the feature $[+Q]$ on C, let's say that *WH* movement is triggered by another feature on C. The feature is $[+WH]$. Recall that $[+Q]$ triggers "head" movement, the movement of the head T to C, another head position. Phrases aren't heads, so phrases cannot move to/occupy a head position. Rather, they move to the specifier position of the head that triggers the movement of the phrase. Following these proposals, let's say that WHQs involve a complementizer with the following feature composition: $C[+Q, +WH]$. The feature $[+Q]$ will trigger T-to-C movement, and the feature $[+WH]$ will trigger the movement of a *wh* phrase to Spec of CP. Applying these movements uniformly to object WHQs such as (3a) and to subject WHQs such as (3d) results in the derivations seen in (4) and (5), respectively.

In (3a/4a), T is only an affix, and no auxiliary verb is present in the structure. The feature $[+Q]$ on C triggers T-to-C movement, as in (4b). Next, the feature $[+WH]$ on C triggers the movement of the *wh* phrase *what* to Spec of CP, as in (4c). Since the tense affix is "stranded" (cut off from the verb by the subject) and cannot undergo Affix Hopping, *Do*-Support applies, resulting in (4d).

As the derivation (5) shows, the same rules of T-to-C movement and *WH* movement apply in the derivation of (3d), but with a very different surface-order result, explaining the very striking difference in the surface word order of complement/adjunct WHQs vs. subject WHQs.

(4)

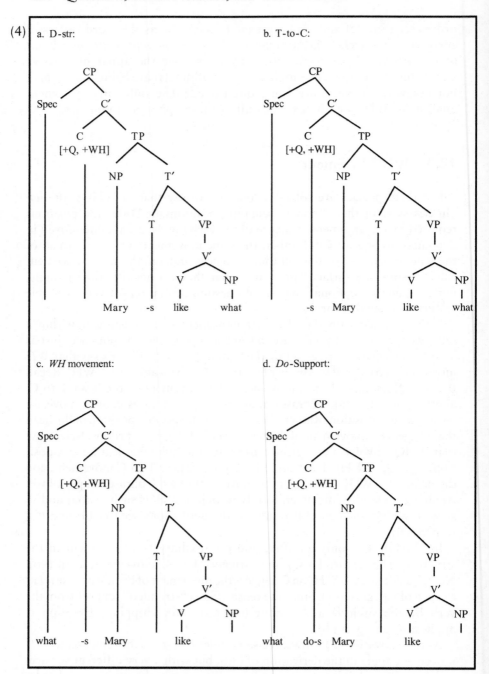

(5)

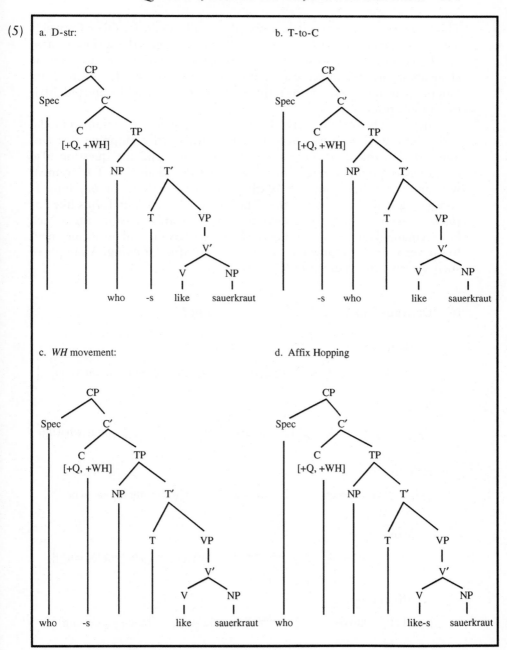

a. D-str:

b. T-to-C

c. *WH* movement:

d. Affix Hopping

This sentence also starts with the tense affix *-s* in T. Again, [+ Q] on C triggers T-to-C movement, as in (5b). Then [+ WH] on C triggers the *WH* movement of *who* to Spec of CP, as in (5c). Notice that in (5c), there are no phonetic elements separating the tense affix in C from the verb *like*. Therefore, Affix Hopping can apply here; it affixes the tense affix to the verb *like*, and (3d/5d) is the surface result.

Other WHQs work similarly. In (3b) and (3c), where T contains a modal verb, the modal verb moves to C, and neither Affix Hopping nor *Do-*Support is invoked. If T contains a tense affix, and the question also contains an auxiliary verb (*have -en* or *be -ing*), then V-to-T movement will apply first and put the auxiliary verb base (*have* or *be*) into T, combining it with the tense affix. Then T, now containing forms like *has* (*have* + *-s*) or *is* (*be* + *-s*), moves to C, and the affixes *-en* or *-ing*, which have remained unmoved thus far and consequently are still positioned next to the verb to their immediate right, undergo Affix Hopping. A sample of such a derivation is given in (6):

(6) **Derivation of *What has Mary been eating?***

  a. D-str:

[$_{CP}$[$_C$[+ Q], [+ WH]] [$_{TP}$ Mary [$_T$-s] [$_{VP}$ have -en[$_{VP}$ be -ing [$_{VP}$ eat what]]]]]]

  b. V-to-T:

[$_{CP}$[$_C$[+ Q], [+ WH]] [$_{TP}$ Mary [$_T$ have-s] [$_{VP}$ -en [$_{VP}$ be-ing [$_{VP}$ eat what]]]]]]

  c. T-to-C:

[$_{CP}$[$_C$[$_T$ have-s] [+Q], [+ WH]] [$_{TP}$ Mary [$_{VP}$-en [$_{VP}$ be-ing [$_{VP}$ eat what]]]]]]

  d. Move *WH*:

[$_{CP}$what [$_C$[$_T$ have-s] [+Q], [+WH]] [$_{TP}$ Mary[$_{VP}$-en[$_{VP}$ be-ing [$_{VP}$ eat]]]]]]

  e. Affix Hopping:

[$_{CP}$ what[$_C$[$_T$ have-s] [+Q], [+WH]] [$_{TP}$ Mary [$_{VP}$ [$_{VP}$ be-en [$_{VP}$ eat-ing]]]]]]

What we have seen is that all of the rules, including T-to-C movement and *WH* movement, apply in a uniform fashion, but with very different surface order consequences. Although complement and adjunct WHQs appear to radically reorder, whereas subject WHQs do not, both types of questions have undergone the same movements. In all cases, T moves to C, and *wh* phrases move to Spec of CP. Argument structure requirements are met at D-str, all theta roles are properly assigned, and a moved *wh* phrase retains its theta role. We might informally write the rule of *WH* movement as in (7):

(7) **WH movement**
    If C is [+ WH, . . .], then move a *wh* phrase to SpecCP.

(e.g., $[_{CP} [_{SpecCP} \varnothing] \underset{[+WH]}{C} [_{TP} \cdots \underset{[+WH]}{XP} \cdots ==>$

$[_{CP} [_{SpecCP} \underset{[+WH]}{XP}] \underset{[\cancel{+WH}]}{C} [_{TP} ... \varnothing ...)$

$[_{SpecCP} \varnothing]$ in the example designates the empty specifer of CP, which rule (7) fills with XP [+ WH]. The "strikethrough" WH feature of C (=[$\cancel{+WH}$]) indicates that the movement has 'satisfied' this feature of C. This is only a first approximation of question formation and the mechanisms involved.

12.4 Relative Clauses

Relative clauses are full clauses that modify NPs. Examples are the CP portions of (8):

(8) a. [_{NP} The person [_{CP} who Mary likes]] has left.
     b. [_{NP} The girl [_{CP} who won the race]] received the medal.

They appear to be N′ adjuncts, as indicated by the fact that, like adjuncts, they can compile in an NP, as shown in (9).

(9) the person who Mary likes who arrived late ...

Let's say that an NP with a relative clause has a structure as in (10).
    As with WHQs, a relative clause may contain a *wh* phrase that is moved to Spec of CP. (The blank after *likes* denotes the D-str position of *who*.) This looks just like the *WH* movement that we have just seen in WHQs, so we might easily claim that relative clauses are CPs whose C also bears the feature [+ WH]. Unlike the Cs in questions, the C of a relative clause lacks the feature [+ Q], so there is no movement of tenses or auxiliary verbs.

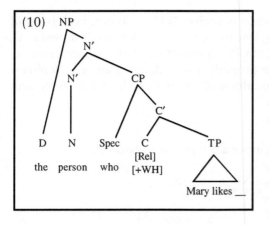

(10)

Relative clauses are worth noting here in part because they help to illustrate an important aspect of the theory being developed. The fact that relative clauses, which are completely distinct from questions, employ *WH* movement shows that the rules of the grammatical system such as *WH* movement are **not construction-specific**. That is, the grammatical system does not employ rules that are dedicated solely to producing a single, specific grammatical construction. For example, *WH* movement is not dedicated to producing only WHQs; rather the process of *WH* movement simply applies anywhere that there is a C with [+ WH] and a *wh* phrase, so it applies in relative clauses, just as it does in WHQs. Likewise, T-to-C movement applies in YNQs just as it does in WHQs, again, two different and distinct constructions. And as we have seen in earlier chapters, *Do*-Support applies in questions as well as in negative sentences and in VP-deletion constructions, as in (11):

(11)   a. What <u>did</u> Mary see?
      b. Mary <u>did</u> not see a flying saucer.
      c. Jane saw a flying saucer, and Mary <u>did</u> too.

Generally, this theory is one of **constructionless syntax**. Specific grammatical constructions such as WHQs, YNQs, relative clauses, negatives, etc. are not of any significance in the grammatical system. They have no actual status or representation there. They are only **epiphenominal** – that is, they are happenstance outcomes of the various smaller features and lexical combinations that can come together and induce the application of very general rules of the system.

As a final observation on relative clauses, note that their form can vary in certain respects. For example, in addition to (8a), it is also possible to say the forms in (12):

(12)   a. [NP The person [CP that Mary likes]] has left.
      b. [NP The person [CP Ø Mary likes]] has left.

It appears that the relative complementizer may appear as *that*. And when it does, then in the place of an overt *wh* phrase, the relative clause employs what is called the **null operator**, in effect, a *wh* phrase with no phonetics. So the structure of (12a) is (13).

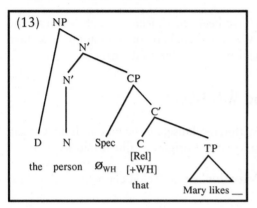

As with a *wh* phrase, the null operator originates in (13) as the object of *like*, and WH movement moves it to Spec of CP.

Both the complementizer and the *wh* phrase have null variants, and it is possible for these to both show up null, as seen in (12b) with the structure (14).

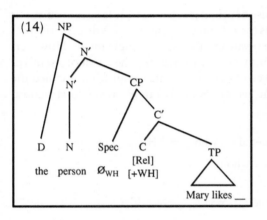

However, the choice among overt and null elements is not completely free. First, while the complementizer and the *wh* phrase may both be null when the *wh* phrase is a complement, they cannot both be null when the *wh* phrase is a subject, as illustrated in (15c):

(15)   a. [NP The person [CP who $\emptyset$C [TP _ likes Max]]] is here

b. [NP The person [CP $\emptyset$WH that [TP _ likes Max]]] is here

c. *[NP The person [CP $\emptyset$WH $\emptyset$C [TP _ likes Max]]] is here

(*The person likes Max is here)

Also, as in (16), Modern English does not allow what has been termed **Doubly-filled Comp**, having both an overt *wh* phrase in Spec of CP and an overt complementizer (though some such constructions are to be found in Middle English):

(16)   a. *The person <u>who that</u> Mary likes _ ...
       b. *The person <u>who that</u> _ likes Max ...

These impossible combinations have been the object of much research and have proven difficult to explain. We note them here, but will not pursue them further, since they entail significantly more advanced work.

12.5   Long Movement and *WH* Islands

A *wh* phrase can move not only within its clause, but beyond it. In fact, it can move indefinitely far away from its site of origin, as illustrated in (17):

(17)   What did Mary say that Max thinks that Zelda claimed ... that Jane bought __ ?

Such movement beyond the clause of origin is referred to as **long movement**. It is tempting to think that perhaps the *wh* phrase simply moves directly from its site of origin to its final surface position, that is, in a single move. However, there is evidence that such long movements are actually the result of a series of short movements. One such piece of evidence comes from what is called the **WH Island Effect**. Consider the sentences in (18) in abbreviated structural form:

(18)   a. $[_{CP} \emptyset_{that} [_{TP}$ Mary wondered $[_{CP}$ who $[_C$ +WH$][_{TP}$ _ saw Jane$]]]]$
       b. $[_{CP}$ Who$[_C$ +WH$[_{TP}$ _ saw who$]]$?
       c. *$[_{CP}$ Who $[_C$ did $[$+WH$]]$
          $[_{TP}$ Mary wonder $[_{CP}$ who $[_C$ +WH $[_{TP}$ _ saw _ $]]]]$?
       d. $[_{CP}$ Who $[_C$ did $[$+WH$]] [_{TP}$ Mary say $[_{CP}$ that $[_{TP}$ Bill saw _ $]]]]$?

Sentence (18a) contains an **embedded question**, the CP *who saw Jane*, which is a complement of the verb *wonder*. The movement of *who* here is just normal *WH* movement within a clause to the embedded Spec of CP. Sentence (18b) shows that it is possible for there to be more than one *wh* phrase in a clause, and when there is, the "higher" one (the one that c-commands the other) moves to Spec of CP – one such movement is enough in English to satisfy the [+ WH] feature of C. Now, if it were possible for *WH* movement to move a *wh* phrase directly to any Spec of CP with C[+ WH], no matter how far away, then it should be possible to say (18c). In (18c), one of the *wh* phrases would have moved to the lower Spec of CP, and the other *wh* phrase to the higher Spec of CP. However, (18c) is strongly unacceptable. This points to the conclusion that simple long *WH* movement must not be possible. Instead, let's say that (i) any *wh* phrase must move only as far as its nearest c-commanding Spec of CP, and (ii) a single Spec of CP position can only accept one moved *wh* phrase (that is, you can't double-fill a single syntactic position). In order to create (18c), we would have to be able to move both *wh* phrases into the single lower Spec of CP position, but since these restrictions disallow such movements, the impossibility of (18c) is explained. So, it looks like any long *WH* movement is actually composed of a series of short moves.

This proposal has a consequence for the analysis of long movement in sentence (18d). If all long *WH* movement is really a series of short movements, and if *WH* movement to Spec of CP is triggered by a feature [+ WH] on C, then it must be that the declarative complementizer *that* in (18d) is capable of bearing a "free" feature [+ WH]. This would allow *who* to get to the lower Spec of CP, and then to be attracted to the next higher Spec of CP by the [+ WH] feature of the higher interrogative C. A more detailed picture of the structure of sentence (18d) is given in (19):

(19) [CP Who[C did[+WH]][TP Mary say [CP – [C that[+WH]][TP Bill saw –]]]]?

In (19), the blanks indicate the path of movement for *who*. First, the "free" [+ WH] feature of *that* triggers the movement of *who* to the lower Spec of CP. Next, the [+ WH] feature of the higher interrogative C triggers the movement of *who* to the higher Spec of CP.

One last question – what if such a "free" feature is assigned to *that*, but there is no *wh* phrase in the structure? We might claim that any such feature must trigger a movement. Such a feature *must* be satisfied. Failure to do so renders the structure "ungrammatical." Thus, such a feature with no *wh* phrase to attract to it will fail.

12.6   Final Remarks

This is just an initial sketch of how WHQs and relative clauses are formed, and of how long movement works. The *WH* Island Effect is only one of a number of island effects that disallow long movement of a *wh* phrase. (The "island" effects are so named because an element that an island construction contains is "marooned" and can't get off/out of the island.) The Spec of CP position that is a "landing site" for *WH* movement is normally termed a "non-argument" position, a position where no "argument" (subject or complement) originates. The positions in which subjects and complements do originate are referred to as "argument positions" or **A-positions**. For contrast, non-argument positions are labeled as **A-bar positions** (or A′ positions). Consequently, any movement to an A-position is referred to as **A movement**, and any movement to an A′ position is referred to as **A′ movement**.

WH movement is an example of A′ movement. In the next chapter, we will investigate a rule of A movement.

Many questions about *WH* movement remain, and there are other possibilities that can be explored in the more advanced literature on this subject, so that is where we will leave things for now.

The grammar with *WH* movement included looks like this:

X-bar syntax
The core architecture:

$$XP \rightarrow (YP), X' \quad \text{(Specifier rule)}$$

$$X' \rightarrow X', WP \quad \text{(Adjunct rule)}$$

$$X' \rightarrow X, (ZP) \quad \text{(Complement rule)}$$

Some additional rules:

$$X^n \rightarrow X^n \text{ Conj } X^n \quad (X^n = \text{any level of X})$$

$$XP \rightarrow \text{ProXP}$$

Some lexical information:

$$T \rightarrow [\text{-}s_{pres}]/[\text{-}ed_{pst}]/[\text{-}\emptyset_{pres}] \quad \text{(These are tense affixes.)}$$

$$\rightarrow [can]/[could]/[will]/[would]/[may]/\text{etc.}$$

$$\rightarrow [to]$$

$$V \rightarrow [have \text{ -en}]/[be \text{ -ing}]/[be \text{ -en}]$$
$$[+Aux]$$

(NB: $\text{-}s_{pres}$, $\text{-}ed_{pst}$, $\text{-}\emptyset_{pres}$, -en, and -ing are $[+affix]$.)

Argument structure: GF interpretation and Argument structure requirements must be satisfied at deep structure.

Head parameter setting: 'head-left' (English)

Some transformations and other devices (stated informally):

V-to-T:
If T is only an affix, then move a following <u>V[+Aux] base</u> to T, and attach the affix to it.

T-to-C: (only in 'root' questions)
Move T to C[+ Q].

WH Movement:
If C is [+ WH, . . .], then move the "nearest" *wh* phrase c-commanded by C to SpecCP (via SpecCP-to-SpecCP in long movements).

Affix Hopping:
"Hop" an affix onto the verb to its immediate right.

"Do"-Support:
Attach "do" to a stranded TNS affix, that is, to a TNS affix that is not to the immediate right of a V and cannot "affix hop" onto it.

Summary Points of This Chapter

- **Object/adjunct WHQs** show very different surface word order from that of **subject WHQs**.
- A rule of obligatory **WH movement**, along with the other rules established thus far, offers a **single, uniform analysis** of both of these types of WHQs.
- In contrast to **head movement**, where a head moves to a c-commanding head position (e.g. V-to-T movement, or T-to-C movement), *WH* movement is an instance of **phrase movement**, where the feature of a head attracts the affected phrase to its Spec position.
- **Relative clauses**, like WHQs, employ *WH* movement, offering evidence that the grammatical system is one of **constructionless syntax**. That is, particular grammatical constructions have no direct representation in the grammatical system.
- *WH* movement offers another instance where **movement is feature-driven**. It is possible that all movements in language are driven by the features of lexical heads.
- *Wh* phrases may undergo **long movement**, movement of an indeterminate distance away from their clause of origin.
- Evidence involving the **WH Island Effect** points toward the conclusion that any long movement is actually the result of a series of short movements.

Problems

1. The grammar with *WH* movement included would analyze the D-str of the sentence "*What is the postman bringing?*" as follows:

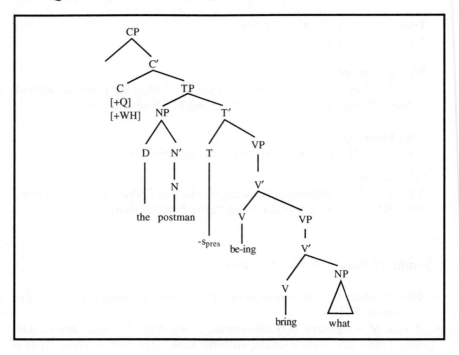

To reach S-str, certain of the transformational rules would apply as follows:

First, V-to-T moves *be* to T.
Next, C[+ Q] triggers T-to-C movement of *is* in T (= *be* + *-s_{pres}*) to C.
Next, C[+ WH] triggers *WH* movement of *what* to Spec of CP.
Finally, Affix Hopping moves *-ing* onto the verb *bring*.

Following this example, draw the D-str tree for each of the following object or adjunct WHQs, and state how each relevant transformational rule applies to derive its S-str. Also, indicate in the D-str tree the GF of any adjuncts and the theta roles of all arguments. (As in this and earlier examples, treat any "D"s and "Quan"s as the simple content of Spec of NP and Spec of VP, respectively, as in the above example.)

a. What does Bill cook?
b. Where has Mary put the tools?
c. Where would Mary like the cups?
d. When is the train from Boston arriving?
e. What did Mary not bring?

2. Next, draw the D-str tree for each of the following subject WHQs, and state how each relevant transformational rule applies to derive its S-str. Here too, indicate in the D-str tree the GF of any adjuncts and the theta roles of all arguments.

    a. Who eats rattlesnake?
    b. Who has been visiting the farm?
    c. Who did not visit the neighbors ?
    d. Who could have been singing?

3. Below is a mix of questions. Again, draw the D-str tree for each of these questions, and state how each relevant transformational rule applies to derive its S-str. Here too, indicate in the D-str tree the GF of any adjuncts and the theta roles of all arguments.

    a. Did they not see the problem?
    b. What is Mary putting on the shelf?
    c. What is Mary a student of?
        (Treat *be* here as a "main verb" with an NP complement (with the theta role "attribute"), but also as bearing the feature [+ Aux], so that it will undergo V-to-T movement.)
    d. Which train has she arrived on?
        (Simply "triangle" the NP *which train*.)

4. Draw the D-str tree for the following NPs containing relative clauses, and state how each relevant transformational rule applies to derive its S-str. Again, indicate in the D-str tree the GF of any adjuncts and the theta roles of all arguments.

    a. the person who Mary has been visiting
    b. the student of music who likes football
    c. the student with long hair that Mary likes
    d. the game which Mary said that Max played
        (Here, *which* is the *wh* phrase used in relative clauses in place of the *what* that would appear in a WHQ.)

5. It was argued earlier that a grammar without a rule of WH movement would encounter problems with questions such as *What does Mary like?*, and that a rule of WH movement can resolve these problems. Recapitulate this argument as follows:

    a. discuss the problems that are raised by object WHQs for a theory of syntax without WH movement, and then
    b. discuss how the inclusion of the rule of WH movement in the theory resolves each problem.

6. (**Advanced**) As we have seen, a question may be embedded as the complement of certain verbs such as *ask* or *wonder*. In embedded questions, we see *WH* movement, but often not T-to-C movement (e.g. *I wonder what Mary can see*). The lack of T-to-C movement here can be accounted for by claiming that the embedded interrogative C bears [+ WH], but not [+ Q]. Further, when the grammatical system operates on a complex sentence structure, it does so one clause (CP) at a time, starting with the lowest clause and working upward through the structure. This method of applying transformations is called **cyclic rule application**. One indication that this is a desirable approach to rule application is found in long *WH* movement, where *WH* movement must move a *wh* phrase only as far as its immediate Spec of CP. Then on the next cycle, it can move the *wh* phrase to the next higher Spec of CP, and so on until the *wh* phrase reaches its final destination. Given, as we have argued, that any long *WH* movement is composed of a series of short moves within each CP, then the cyclic rule application approach is compatible in the extreme with this analysis of long *WH* movement.

    Following this line of analysis, draw the D-str tree for each of the complex sentences below, and state how each relevant transformational rule applies to derive its S-str. Here too, indicate in the D-str tree the GF of any adjuncts and the theta roles of all arguments.

    a. Mary has wondered what the Martians want.
    b. Bill says that that student of music with long hair is playing a recorder.
    c. Where does Mary think that Max is putting the motorcycle?

7. (**Advanced**) Consider the possible sentences in (i) and (ii), and the possible and impossible relative clauses in (iii) and (iv).

    i. Mary said that Max likes Zelda.
    ii. Mary asked who likes Zelda.
    iii. The person who Mary said that Max likes
    iv. *The person who Mary asked who likes

    a. Do these sentences and relative clauses offer further evidence that relative clauses involve *WH* movement? Explain how they do.
    b. Considering the possible relative clause in (v) and the impossible one in (vi), explain how these relative clauses might be argued to offer evidence that there is indeed a null operator in relative clauses that undergoes *WH* movement.

    v. the person Mary said Max likes
    vi. *the person Mary asked who likes

8. (**Advanced**) Consider the following relative clauses involving coordination:

   i. The boy and the girl who Mary saw.
   (ambiguous, meaning either the girl or both were seen by Mary)
   ii. a boy and a girl with long hair
   (ambiguous, meaning either that the girl or both have long hair)

   Earlier, it was claimed that relative clauses are adjuncts adjoined to N'. Discuss how the above relative clauses point toward broadening the possibilities for adjunct attachment.

13

NP Movement

Next, let's consider the question of where the subjects of sentences originate. First, we'll consider the subjects of active sentences and the **"VP-internal subject" hypothesis,** the idea that semantic subjects originate not in SpecTP, but lower in the structure, in SpecVP. Then we'll consider the puzzle of passive sentences, sentences in which the surface subject has an object meaning. What we will see overall is that what turns up as a surface subject is simply the "nearest" eligible NP that can be attracted to SpecTP without regard to its semantic subject or object status.

13.1   VP-Internal Subjects

In numerous sentences, the subject at the surface resides in SpecTP, as seen in (1):

(1)   All the girls have ordered oysters.

However, certain facts suggest that the subject may in fact originate in a lower position and raise to SpecTP in its derivation to surface form. This is suggested by sentences such as (2):

(2)   The girls have all ordered oysters.

Recall from Chapter 10 that the SpecVP position was claimed to be filled with a subject-related quantifier such as *each* or *all*, as in sentence (2). This phenomenon of a subject-related quantifier being physically separated from

Syntactic Analysis: *The Basics*   Nicholas Sobin
© 2011 Nicholas Sobin

the subject is known as **quantifier floating**. We might wonder why subject-related material would appear in a lower position than the rest of the subject. A possible answer is that the entire subject originates in the SpecVP position, and in moving up toward SpecTP, it may "break up" and leave the quantifier behind. Under this hypothesis, (1) and (2) would share the D-str shown in (3).

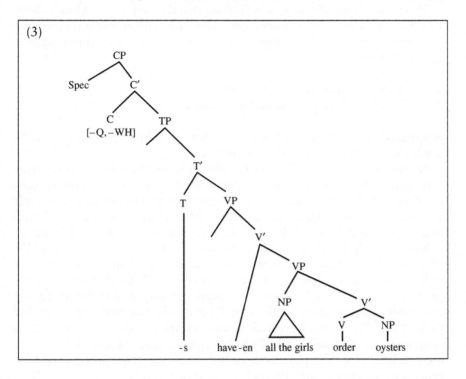

(3)

In fact, if we consider a sentence with a more elaborated auxiliary verb sequence such as (4) below, it becomes apparent that a quantifier may be "left behind" in any of the Spec positions between the lowest Spec of VP and Spec of TP, the surface subject position. In (4), the quantifier *all* may appear in any one (and *only* one) of the parenthesized positions.

(4) (All) the girls could (all) have (all) been (all) buying postcards.

Since each of the verbs in (4) heads a VP, and since X-bar theory projects the possible presence of a Spec position for each of these VPs, it looks as though the subject moves through each SpecVP until it reaches SpecTP. (I leave it to the reader to draw the relevant tree and verify this.) We might say that the head T "attracts" an NP to its Spec position, but that such movement must proceed one Spec at a time through each of the intervening empty Spec positions. That is, this sort of NP movement is always **local movement** – movement to the next immediately c-commanding Spec position until the final target is reached. There has been a lot of debate about why the subject "stops off" in each of the intervening Spec positions within the clause. We'll leave that topic as one for later study.

There are further advantages to thinking that the subject starts low, in Spec VP. For one, in **expletive constructions** (sentences with an expletive pronoun such as *there* for a surface subject) as in (5b), the semantic subject actually appears low on the surface.

(5)   a. <u>Some birds</u> have been singing.
      b. There have been <u>some birds</u> singing.

It appears that if *there* is chosen to appear in subject position, then the semantic subject stays low in the structure.

Another advantage for VP-internal subjects is that the subject is close to the verb that assigns its theta role, just as objects are. If it were more distant, the verb would have to look past auxiliary verb material that is irrelevant to theta role assignment to theta mark its subject. But with the subject starting in SpecVP, all of the verb's arguments are local to the verb, that is, within the VP domain.

Now, let's deal with the question of why the subject moves to SpecTP – what might it be that triggers such movement? Recall that in the analysis of WHQs, it was claimed that C bears a feature [+WH] that attracts a *wh* phrase to SpecCP. If features of a head are responsible for triggering movement, then we might claim that T bears a feature that attracts an NP to SpecTP. This feature has had various names in various theories. Let's simply call the feature [+N]. With the understanding that such movement must be local (Spec-to-Spec), as described above, we might propose a rule or process of movement that affects NPs, as stated in (6):

(6)   **NP movement**

   T[+N] attracts the "nearest" NP that it c-commands to the "empty" subject (SpecTP) position via "local" Spec-to-Spec movement. E.g.,

$$[_{TP} [_{SpecTP} \emptyset] \underset{[+N]}{T} \ldots [_{VP} \ldots NP \ldots] \ldots] \Rightarrow$$

$$[_{TP} [_{SpecTP} NP] \underset{[+N]}{T} \ldots [_{VP} \ldots \emptyset_{NP} \ldots] \ldots]$$

Such a rule would find the NP *all the girls* in tree (3) and trigger its movement through the SpecVP of *have* to Spec TP, with the possibility that the NP might "break up," leaving the quantifier *all* in some Spec along the movement path, as seen for example in (2). Of course there is much more to be explained about why such NPs can drop the quantifier, but we reserve that topic as one for a more advanced study.

13.2 Passive Sentences I: Apparent Problems

Passive sentences are ones like (7b) and (8b):

(7) a. Max saw Mary in Berlin. (active)
    b. Mary was seen in Berlin (by Max). (passive)

(8) a. Jane gave a book to Mary. (active)
    b. A book was given to Mary (by Jane). (passive)

Such sentences present challenges to any theory of sentence structure, as outlined in (9):

(9)   **Problems posed by passive sentences**
    a. The surface subject has an object meaning. How can an object theta role be assigned to an apparent subject?
    b. There is a "hole" in the structure where the object ought to be – an apparent argument structure violation. How can argument structure violations be allowed?
    c. The complement of *by* has a subject meaning. How can a subject theta role be assigned to the object of a preposition?
    d. The *by*-phrase containing the subject is optional. Normally, English subjects are required and not omissible. Why is the subject expression omissible here?

We can begin an analysis by considering the sentences in (10):

(10) a. Mary chose Max.
     b. Mary <u>was</u> chos<u>en</u> by Max.

The sentences in (10) are a sort of syntactic "minimal pair," differing by active vs. passive features. In (10a), *Mary* is the agent, and *Max* is the *theme*. And despite the fact that *Mary* and *Max* are in the same relative order in (10b), we understand *Mary* to be the theme, and *Max* to be the agent. The only morphological cue that these interpretations should be "reversed" in (10b) is the presence of what we will term **passive morphology** in (10b) – the auxiliary verb [*be -en*] which is present in a passive sentence. Before proceeding to an analysis of passive, it is helpful to briefly consider Case, which has often been considered a central factor in the analysis of passive sentences. Case will not be as central here as it has been claimed to be in certain past analyses, but it is nonetheless significant and warrants some brief discussion.

13.3   A Sketch of Case

Case refers to the form that NPs assume depending on their surface structural positioning. In Modern English, Case forms are restricted largely to pronouns (ProNPs). In a simple active sentence with a finite tense such as (11), the subject *she* is a **nominative** Case form, and the object *her* is an **accusative** Case form:

(11)   She saw her.

In such sentences, subjects are typically nominative and objects are typically accusative. The various Case forms are exemplified in (12):

(12)   **Case and forms**

Nominative: I, we, she, he, they, . . .
Accusative: me, us, her, him, them, . . .
Genitive: my, your, his, her, their, . . .
Genitive replacive: mine, yours, his, hers, theirs, . . .

In Old English, and still in Modern German, not just pronouns but all NPs exhibit Case forms. The masculine Case forms of Modern German are illustrated in (13):

(13)   **(Masculine) Case forms of German 'the man' and 'he' etc:**

Nominative:	der Mann;	er (= he)
Genitive:	des Mannes;	sein (= his)
Dative:	dem Mann;	ihm (= (to) him)
Accusative	den Mann;	ihn (= him)

Note that in German, Case is marked largely on the determiner, except for genitive, which also marks the noun. Interestingly, this Case form has been retained in modern English, and still appears on NPs, as illustrated in (14):

(14)   **English NPs show genitive**

[$_{NP}$ [$_{NP}$ the girl] -'s$_{poss}$ hat]

Notice also that the English accusative *-m* (used for what would be both accusative and dative in German) (*him*, *them*, *whom*) comes from the Germanic dative.

We might wonder why it is basically in pronouns that Case marking has been preserved in English. One reason may be that pronouns are a closed class category and don't participate in any productive morphology, so they are in effect "memorized" forms anyway. Thus, there may have been little reason for them to undergo any radical change. However, there is still the fact that NPs get Case marked in genitive (possessive) constructions. A theory that has some currency is one that argues that in fact all NPs necessarily undergo Case marking, and that Case marking (like the present tense affix on non-3rd-person-singular verbs) has simply lost its phonetic manifestation on NPs (except for the genitive -*s*). Thus, it isn't just the pronouns that get Case marked – every NP undergoes Case marking. The NP complements (objects) of verbs are Case marked by the verb, and the object of a preposition is Case marked by the preposition. This sort of Case is called **abstract Case**, since it is often not manifest phonetically. The Cases that appear phonetically on the surface are referred to as **morphological Case**. Theoretical linguistics has been crucially interested in abstract Case, and when we refer to Case from here on, that is what we will mean.

We have not yet mentioned the Case on subject NPs. In English, the subject of a **finite clause** (a clause whose T is a present or past tense affix, or a modal verb) is nominative. It appears to be **finite T** that assigns nominative Case to the NP that appears in subject position. Let's say that finite T assigns nominative to the nearest NP that it c-commands, and it is that NP which is attracted by T[+ N] to the SpecTP position. This idea will interact neatly with the analysis of passives to be presented below.

In sum, an object NP gets Case marked by the nearest c-commanding V or P, usually the V or P that selected it as a complement. A subject NP gets its Case from finite T. What is termed the **Case Filter** embodies the idea that a sentence "crashes" (is declared ungrammatical) if it surfaces containing an NP without a Case. There is much more to be said about Case, and many refinements to be made to the preceding analysis, but for our purposes here, this much is sufficient to deal with an initial analysis of passive sentences.

13.4   Passive Sentences II: An Analysis

Based on work by Chomsky and many others, the apparently odd behaviors of passive sentences noted in (9) might be explained as outlined in (15):

(15)   **Analysis of passive sentences**

   a. Passive morphology 'absorbs' the accusative Case of the verb, so that the passive verb has no accusative Case to assign to its complement.
   b. Passive morphology "suppresses" the subject theta role of the verb; that is, it curtails the verb's ability to assign its subject theta role to

an NP in SpecVP position, forcing this position to start out empty. (If it were filled, there would be a Theta Criterion violation.)

c. The rule Move NP simply works here as it does elsewhere. Since a subject NP does not appear in SpecVP of a passive verb, T[+N] seeks the "nearest" NP that it c-commands, attracting it to SpecTP (via Spec-to-Spec movement). In a passive sentence, that NP will be the nearest object.

d. The *by*-phrase is a V' adjunct phrase; *by* signals that its object should get the "suppressed" subject theta role of the verb.

To spell this out a bit more, the deep structure of a passive sentence such as (16a) is (16b).

(16)   a. Mary was visited by Martians.

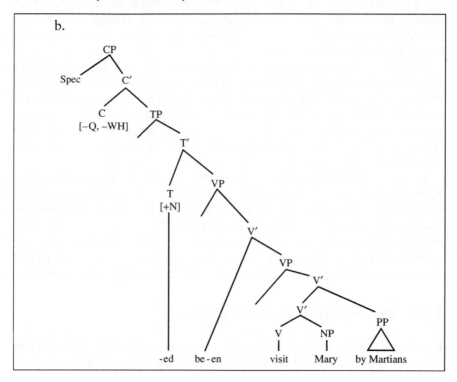

In (16b), the subject position (SpecVP) is empty. Passive morphology (*be -en*) has suppressed the verb's ability to assign its subject theta role to an NP originating in this position, so none may appear. By a process that is labeled **argument demotion**, the verb may assign the subject theta role to an adjunct. For compatibility, the adjunct must be headed by a word that itself can assign that theta role to its complement NP. Here, the preposition *by* fulfills that role. Consider NPs such as the one in (17):

(17)   a sonata by Mozart

Even lacking a sentence context, we understand Mozart in (17) to be an agent, the composer (or possibly player) of the sonata. Thus, the subject theta role of *visit* in (16) is assigned to the adjunct PP *by Martians*, whose head *by* is a compatible agent assigner, and can transmit the subject theta role to its complement NP *Martians*. Assuming that a suppressed theta role may be but does not have to be expressed, the *by*-phrase is optional and need not appear in a passive sentence.

Passive morphology also absorbs the accusative Case that *visit* would have assigned to its complement NP *Mary*, so this NP will need to get a Case from somewhere else. T[+ N] looks for the nearest NP that it c-commands. It finds *Mary*, assigns it nominative Case, and pulls it up (via Spec-to-Spec movement) to SpecTP. Notice that the correct pronoun form of *Mary* in (16) is *she* (nominative) and not *her* (accusative), confirming that *Mary* is getting nominative Case. The other rules apply in the usual way. V-to-T will combine *be* with T, and Affix Hopping will place *-en* on the verb to its right, *visit*, producing the past participle verb form *visited*. Thus we get sentence (16a), with the subject position containing an NP with object meaning, and an adjunct phrase containing the semantic subject.

What is interesting and rather compelling about this analysis is its high degree of generality. As different as passive sentences appear to be from active ones (as sketched in (9) above), there are no separate rules of syntax for passives. The very same rules of syntax are used to form both active and passive sentences. Passive sentences only differ from active ones in their morphology. Passive morphology alters what the verb can do (subject theta role suppression and accusative Case absorption), and the syntax simply operates as usual, given these alterations. That is a neat result. The process of NP movement, which transports an NP ultimately to Spec of TP is, like WH movement, **not construction-specific**. It participates in the derivation of both active and passive sentences. For convenience, we repeat the rule of NP movement here as (18):

(18)   **NP Movement** $(= (6))$
       T[+ N] attracts the "nearest" NP that it c-commands to the "empty" subject (SpecTP) position via "local" Spec-to-Spec movement. E.g.,

$$[_{TP} [_{SpecTP} \emptyset] \underset{[+N]}{T} \ldots [_{VP} \ldots NP \ldots] \ldots] \Rightarrow$$

$$[_{TP} [_{SpecTP} NP] \underset{[+N]}{T} \ldots [_{VP} \ldots \emptyset_{NP} \ldots] \ldots]$$

13.5   Subject-to-Subject Raising

Another construction that utilizes NP movement is exemplified in (19b) and (20b):

(19) a. It seems that Mary   (*Mary* = "experiencer" of *like*)
          likes sauerkraut.

      b. Mary seems to like sauerkraut.   (*Mary* = "experiencer" of *like*)

(20) a. It is likely that Mary will leave.   (*Mary* = "agent" of *leave*)

      b. Mary is likely to leave.   (*Mary* = "agent" of *leave*)

In (19a) and (20a), *Mary* is the subject of the embedded clause and nothing more. Further, (19a) and (19b) have the same meaning, as do (20a) and (20b). Therefore, although *Mary* is positioned in (19b) and (20b) as the subject of the matrix clause, in fact, it bears only the subject theta role of the embedded clause. How is this to be explained?

Given the grammatical system that we have established thus far, this can be explained largely in terms of the argument structure of the main verb/ adjective expressions *seem* and *(be) likely*, shown in (21) and (22), respectively:

(21) *seem*, V, . . . ,   Args: Cats: Theta roles:
                             1   –   –
                             2   CP(fin)/TP(inf)   theme

(22) *(be) likely*, Aj, . . .   Args: Cats: Theta roles:
                                1   –   –
                                2   CP(fin)/TP(inf)   theme

Seem and *(be) likely* in (21) and (22), do not specify the type subject, nor do they assign it a theta role. Any possible subject of the clause complement of *seem/(be) likely* can appear in the subject position of *seem*, as in (23):

(23) a. It seems that [in the bathtub] is the safest place in a tornado.
      b. [In the bathtub] seems to be the safest place in a tornado.
      c. It seems that [taking the train] is easy.
      d. [Taking the train] seems to be easy.
      e. ??It seemed that [that Mary had left] was a problem.
      f. [That Mary had left] seemed to be a problem.

Hence, either an expletive pronoun (*it*, which has no meaning) appears as the subject of these expressions, as in (19a) and (20a), or an NP from another position will move into the matrix subject position, bringing its own theta role with it. This is what we are seeing in (19b) and (20b).

In more detail, consider first the D-str (24) for sentence (19a). As noted in (24), transitive verbs such as *like* have an accusative Case to assign to their complements, and finite tense affixes have a nominative Case to assign to a subject. Here, *seem* has selected a finite CP as its complement. In the lower CP, *Mary* will be attracted by T[+ N] to Spec of TP (NP movement), and T will assign *Mary* nominative Case. The lower tense affix -*s* will Affix Hop onto the verb *like*. Then in the higher CP, the tense affix -*s* will Affix Hop onto the verb *seem*. But what about a subject for *seem*?

(24)

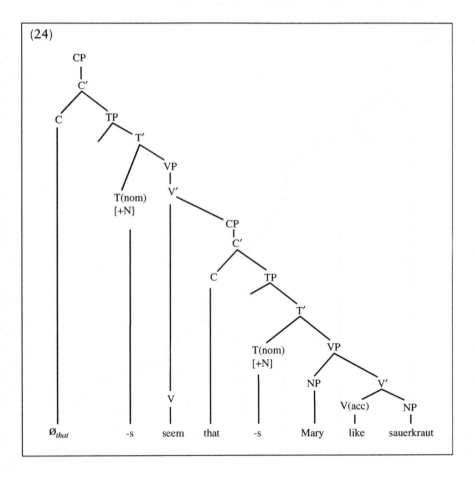

At this point, let's add one more important detail, something that we will call the **CP Extraction Condition**, which is given in (25). (This is a very preliminary version of Chomsky's "Phase Impenetrability Condition," which you will encounter in later work.)

(25)   **The CP Extraction Condition**
Only an element located in Spec of CP may be extracted (moved) out of an embedded CP directly into a higher CP.

Thus in (24), the T[+ N] in the higher CP cannot attract *Mary*, since it is not located in Spec of CP, but further down, inside the lower TP. Therefore, the only choice for filling the higher subject position and satisfying the [+ N] feature of the higher T is to insert the expletive pronoun *it*. The result is sentence (19a).
Sentence (19b) has the somewhat different D-str in (26).

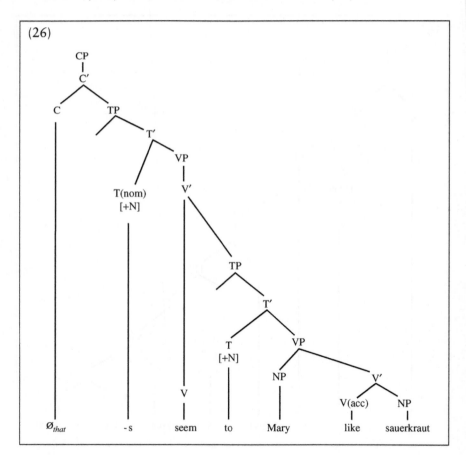

(26)

Here, *seem* has selected its other possible complement type, an infinitival TP, not a full CP. In an infinitival TP, T is realized as *to*, the infinitival particle that often accompanies uninflected verbs in English (e.g. *to like*). In the lower TP, *Mary* will be attracted by T[+ N] to Spec of TP (NP movement), but T will not assign *Mary* a Case, since infinitival T (*to*) has no Case to assign. In the higher CP, T[+ N] is allowed to attract *Mary* from its position in the lower Spec of TP to the higher Spec of TP (another instance of NP movement). This is because the CP Extraction Condition will not be violated – we are not attempting movement out of an embedded CP. This higher T is finite, and so it has a nominative Case, which it will assign to *Mary*. The tense affix *-s* will Affix Hop onto the verb *seem*, and the result is sentence (19b).

13.6 Summary Remarks

In this chapter, we've considered the idea that the subjects of sentences do not originate in their surface position, but further down in the structure. "Active" subjects originate in Spec of VP, "passive" subjects originate in a non-subject position, and some verbs such as *seem* go so far as to "steal" the subject or complement of another clause. Common to all of these various constructions is the rule of NP movement. This further supports the idea that rules/processes involved in sentence production are construction-neutral. That is, particular syntactic constructions are a by-product of the grammatical system. They are not directly encoded or represented ("known") in the speaker's internalized system of grammar. In an important sense, they are not "real."

The grammar that we have developed thus far with NP movement included looks like this:

Summary Grammar

The core X-bar architecture:

$$XP \rightarrow (YP),\ X' \quad \text{(Specifier rule)}$$
$$X' \rightarrow X',\ WP \quad \text{(Adjunct rule)}$$
$$X' \rightarrow X,\ (ZP) \quad \text{(Complement rule)}$$

Some additional rules:

$$X^n \rightarrow X^n\,\text{Conj}\,X^n \quad (X^n = \text{any level of X})$$
$$XP \rightarrow \text{ProXP}$$

Some lexical information:

T	→	$[-s_{pres}]/[-ed_{pst}]/[-\emptyset_{pres}]$	(These are tense affixes.)
	→	$[can]/[could]/[will]/[would]/[may]$etc.	
	→	$[to]$	
V	→	$[have\ -en]/[be\ -ing]/[be\ -en]$	
$[+Aux]$			

(NB : $-s_{pres}$, $-ed_{pst}$, $-\emptyset_{pres}$, $-en$, and $-ing$ are $[+affix]$.)

Argument structure: GF interpretation and Argument structure requirements must be satisfied at deep structure.

Head parameter setting: "head-left" (English)

Some transformations and other devices (stated informally):

The CP Extraction Condition:
Only an element located in Spec of CP may be extracted (moved) out of an embedded CP directly into a higher CP.

NP Movement:
If T is $[+N, \ldots]$, move the "nearest" NP c-commanded by T to SpecTP (via Spec-to-Spec movement).

V-to-T:
If T is only an affix, then move a following $V[+Aux]$ base to T, and attach the affix to it.

T-to-C: (only in "root" questions)
Move T to $C[+Q]$.

WH Movement:
If C is $[+WH, \ldots]$, then move the "nearest" *wh* phrase c-commanded by C to SpecCP (via SpecCP-to-SpecCP in long movements).

Affix Hopping:
"Hop" an affix onto the verb to its immediate right.

"Do"-Support:
Attach "do" to a stranded tense affix, that is, to a tense affix that is not to the immediate right of a V and cannot "affix hop" onto it.

Summary Points of This Chapter

- The phenomenon of **quantifier floating** and the low subjects seen in **expletive constructions** point toward the possibility that the subject of an "active" sentence **may originate low in the structure, in Spec of VP.**
- **NP movement** is triggered by a feature [+ N] on a c-commanding T. Thus, like *WH* movement, NP movement is **feature-driven.**
- NP movement moves an "active" subject NP from Spec of VP **through each intervening Spec position** (as quantifier floating facts indicate) **to Spec of TP**, the surface position of subjects.
- **"Passive" sentences**, whose subject is normally the object/complement of the verb, display some very clear surface indications of a "moved" subject. The immediate utility of NP movement in passive sentences adds further support to the **general NP movement hypothesis**, the hypothesis that lexical subjects do not originate in surface subject position, but rather are moved there from a variety of lower positions.
- **Subject-to-subject raising constructions**, which can actually "steal" the subject of another clause, offer further dramatic evidence for the general NP movement hypothesis.
- NP movement is restricted by the **CP Extraction Condition**, which bars extraction of an element from anywhere in an embedded CP except Spec of CP.
- NP movement is, therefore, **not construction-specific.** The rules of the grammatical system appear not to encode grammatical constructions per se. A speaker does not "know" them, even subconsciously, just as a speaker does not "know" a particular sentence or a particular number, for that matter.
- **Morphological Case** is the surface Case form assigned to an NP or ProNP depending on its surface position in a sentence.
- The **Abstract Case hypothesis** says that all lexical NPs are assigned a Case, whether or not it is manifest in their surface form. The **Case Filter** says that any sentence containing a lexical NP that is not Case marked at surface structure is declared ungrammatical.

Problems

1. Low subject active sentences. Assuming that subjects originate in and have their subject theta roles assigned in SpecVP of the main verb, draw the D-str tree for each of the following active sentences, and state how each relevant transformational rule applies to derive its S-str. Indicate in the D-str tree the GF of any adjuncts and the theta roles of all arguments.

    a. Mary spotted a T-rex.
    b. Max is giving Mary a book.
    c. Mary could have been playing folk songs
    d. There could have been birds singing.
       (Assume that *there*, like the *it* of "*It seems*...", is inserted late if NP isn't
       moved to satisfy T[+N].)
    e. The birds could have all been singing.

2. Simple passives. Draw the D-str for each of the following sentences, and
    state how each relevant transformational rule applies to derive its S-str.
    Here too, indicate in the D-str tree the GF of any adjuncts and the theta
    roles of all arguments.

    a. A T-rex was spotted!
    b. Was Mary given a book?
    c. The tree was damaged by the wind.
    d. The book on the table is liked by everyone.
    e. The book is liked by everyone in the room.
    f. Could that book have been being read by everyone?

3. Interrogative and negative passives. Draw the D-str for each of the
    following sentences, and state how each relevant transformational rule
    applies to derive its S-str. Indicate in the D-str tree the GF of any adjuncts
    and the theta roles of all arguments.

    a. Who was visited by her?
    b. Who was the soup made by?
    c. Who has been given a book?
    d. Who was not given a book?
    e. What has not been seen by everyone?
    f. Was Mary not told the whole story?
    g. When was Mary visited by Martians?

4. Subject-to-subject-raising sentences. Draw the D-str for each of the
    following sentences, and state how each relevant transformational rule
    applies to derive its S-str. Indicate in the D-str tree the GF of any adjuncts
    and the theta roles of all arguments.

    a. It seems that they have all taken their seats. (Treat *their* as a D.)
    b. The people seem to have all taken their seats.
    c. Mary seems to have been given a prize.
    d. Mary appears not to be taking the bait. (*Appear* works like *seem*.)
    e. The people appear not to be all taking the bait.

5. Recapitulate the argument that in passive sentences, the surface subject has originated in a complement position. First state the facts, and then state the conclusion that these facts point toward.

6. Recapitulate the argument that in what we have called subject-to-subject-raising sentences, the subject has come from a lower clause. First state the facts, and then state the conclusion that these facts point toward.

7. (**Advanced**) Given that we appear to need NP movement to explain the facts of passive and subject-to-subject-raising sentences, if we had not yet considered active sentences, how does this lend further credence to the proposal that active sentences also have "raised" subjects?

14

Things to Come
Various Aspects of "Current Theory"

This has been a brief introduction to some of the whats and whys fundamental to the study of modern generative syntax. Though we've dealt with a number of significant aspects of this field, there are many others that remain and that will have to await a more extensive study. We will mention a few of them briefly here.

14.1 Unaccusative Verbs

Some verbs that we have (or would have) treated thus far as having a subject originating in SpecVP have been argued instead to have their surface subjects originate in a complement-of-V position. Consider the sentences in (1):

(1) a. The Bismarck sank.
     b. We sank the Bismarck.
     c. The Bismarck sank, and we did it.

Say that you were a British crewperson on the HMS *Rodney* or the HMS *King George V*. In claiming to have sunk the *Bismarck*, you might have uttered sentence (1c). What is surprising about (1c) is that though the superficial referent of *it* appears to be *the Bismarck sank*, what's really being expressed is (1b). To resolve this puzzle, note that *the Bismarck* in (1a) and (1b) seems to have the same "patient" theta role with respect to *sink*, despite the fact that it looks like a subject in (1a) and a complement in (1b). Such verbs as *sink* in (1a) are said to be **unaccusative**. They have no subject theta role (like a passive

Syntactic Analysis: *The Basics*   Nicholas Sobin
© 2011 Nicholas Sobin

verb), and hence lack a subject in D-str. They are labeled unaccusative because (again like a passive verb), while they are transitive and theta mark a complement, they lack an accusative Case to assign to that complement. Thus, in (1a), NP movement raises the object to its surface subject position in SpecTP. (Yet more work for NP movement!)

This analysis comprises the **unaccusative hypothesis**, the hypothesis that certain "active" verbs have a surface subject originating from a complement position. Not all intransitive verbs lack real subjects. Verbs such as *smile* have a true agent subject, and are referred to as **unergative**.

14.2   VP Shells and Verb Raising

Thus far, we have treated VPs containing more than one complement as though they had a "flat" structure (e.g. [$_{V'}$ V NP NP]). However, certain key facts suggest that in a VP with two complements, these complements are asymmetrical – the first c-commands the second, but not vice versa. Consider the following sentences:

(2)   a. Mary told no one anything.
      b. *Mary told anyone nothing.

(3)   a. We gave him himself.   (how a person might be 'freed' from slavery)
      b. *We gave himself him.

(4)   a. Mary told nothing to anyone.
      b. *Mary told anything to no one.

(5)   a. We gave him to himself.
      b. *We gave himself to him.

The sentences of (2) and (4) involve negative polarity items (NPIs – see Chapter 7). Recall that an NPI must be c-commanded by a negative element. If the structure of V′ in (2) were flat, then both (2a) and (2b) should be equally possible, but they are not. It appears then that the first complement c-commands the second, but not vice versa. Similarly, the sentences in (3) and (5) involve reflexives and pronominals governed by Principles A and B, respectively. Again, if the structure of V′ were flat, (3a) should be impossible as a Principle B violation, but it is not. Thus, while *him* must c-command and bind *himself* to comply with Principle A, it must also be true that *himself* does not c-command *him*, in compliance with Principle B.

A further curiosity is that the two complements, while not forming any sort of single referential entity, nonetheless appear to form a constituent that may be coordinated, as in (6):

(6)   a. Mary told [Zelda one story] and [Jane another].
      b. Mary gave [Henry a toy train] and [Luke a toy bus].
      c. Mary told [one story to Zelda] and [another to Jane].
      d. Mary gave [a toy train to Henry] and [a toy bus to Luke].

The **VP shell hypothesis** addresses these questions. For sentences with an NP and PP complement combination such as *Mary told a story to Zelda* (like those in (4–5) and in (6c–d)), it posits the VP structure in (7).

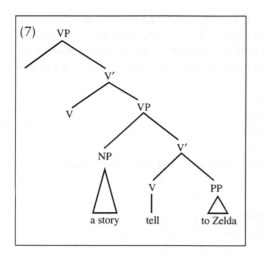

The lower VP headed by the main verb takes the "indirect object" as its immediate complement, and the "direct object" complement appears in SpecVP. This VP is the complement to an abstract verb "V" (something that has come to be called "little *v*," but this idea will be developed in future studies), which projects a higher VP, the "VP shell." In derivation, a rule of verb raising raises *tell* to the higher V position, leaving the lower VP with only the two complements, NP and PP. This explains the coordination possibilities in (6c) and (6d).

Next, if we want to maintain the idea that a particular theta role is always assigned to a particular structural position (something known as the **uniform theta assignment hypothesis**, or **UTAH**), then the VP shell analysis of VPs with two NP complements is the one in (8).

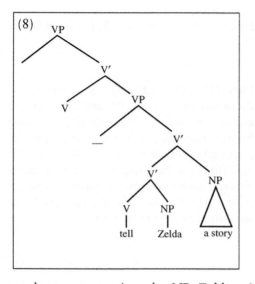

Note that the "indirect object" argument *Zelda* is still the immediate complement of *tell*. This analysis follows along the lines of the analysis of passive sentences. The verb cannot Case mark its object, so if *to* indicates such Case marking, then what would have been a PP *to Zelda* is reduced to a simple NP *Zelda*. The "direct object" complement *a story* has, analogous to the subject of a passive sentence, been demoted to V′ adjunct status and gets the theta role that would have been assigned to the SpecVP position. Also analogous to passive, the NP *Zelda* raises to the empty lower SpecVP position, the verb raises to the higher V position, and we are left with the structure (9).

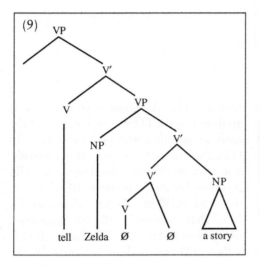

This structure explains the asymmetric c-command relations between the two NP complements, the apparent reversal of order of thematic elements as compared to the NP and PP complement VPs (a phenomenon known as **dative shift**), and the formation of the two NP complements into a coordinatable single constituent, here the lower VP.

14.3 DP vs. NP

To this point we have dealt with the subjects and objects of sentences as NPs. However, it is widely claimed that it is not N, but D that heads such arguments. The structure of an NP such as *that story about Zelda* would be as in (10).

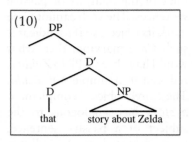

Here, D is the head and NP is its complement. Pronouns such as *she*, *he*, and *they* may be considered ProDPs. Alternatively, they have been characterized as D heads that do not take a complement. We might ask what fills SpecDP. Some have hypothesized that that is the position for possessive phrases, so that the phrase *Mary's story about Zelda* might be structured as in (11) or as in (12).

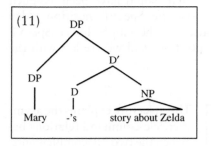

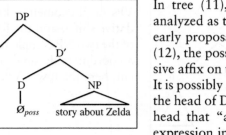

In tree (11), the possessive affix *-'s* is analyzed as the D head of DP, one of the early proposals about possessive DPs. In (12), the possessive *-'s* is simply a possessive affix on the embedded possessor DP. It is possibly an "agreement affix," where the head of DP in (12) is a null possessive head that "agrees" with the possessive expression in SpecDP. The fact that (13) is a possible coordination suggests that (12) rather than (11) may be the correct structure.

(13)   The boy's and the girl's toys (were on the table).

14.4 Conclusion

There is, of course, much more to be said about all of this, and that is one of the fascinating things about this area of inquiry. The ongoing questions about what is forming up in the mind of a three-year-old go deeper and deeper.

Appendix 1

Minor Grammatical Categories

Below is a listing of some prominent minor grammatical categories, along with brief notations on the characteristics and positional criteria that distinguish them.

Negator: *not*

> A one-member category
> Normal positioning is after the first auxiliary verb/morpheme.

Determiner (Article):

- Definite: *the*
- Indefinite: *a(n)*
- Demonstratives: *this, that, these, those*
- Quantifiers: *all, some, many, few, much, little, each, every, more, most, fewer, less, least, any, several, no,* etc.

Generally, any of these elements will serve the function of a determiner (e.g., *a book, the book, this book, each book* (cf. *[NP book])), though there are ordering complexities among them (e.g., all the more food). Normal position is at the left periphery of NP.

Auxiliary verb:

- Non-modal: *have -en* (Perfective), *be -ing* (Progressive), *be -en* (Passive)
- Modal:
  "Present": *will, can, shall, may, must* (also *do, does*))
  "Past": *would, could, should, might* (also *did*)

Syntactic Analysis: *The Basics*   Nicholas Sobin
© 2011 Nicholas Sobin

These occur to the left of a main verb as follows:

(M) (have -en) (be -ing) (be -en)

Tense affixes (*-s* (present) and *-ed* (past)) appear only on the leftmost item. Any left-most Aux verb moves to pre-subject position to form a YNQ.

- Infinitival *to*
  Positions like (and excludes) a modal auxiliary verb (M above).

Intensifiers: *very, quite, rather, awfully, really, plum*

These position to the left of adjectives and adverbs, at the left periphery of AjP (and AvP, if there is such a thing).

Pronouns:

- Ordinary (personal): *I, me, my, mine, you, you, your, yours*, etc.

These vary in form, exhibiting Case marking, as do other pronouns to follow. Also, these pronouns must have a "non-local" referent – they cannot refer to something too near:

$[_S$ Jane$_i$ saw her$_{j/*i}]$

- Reflexive: the *-self/-selves* forms.
- Reciprocal: *each other, one another*, etc.

These two types must have a "local" referent – they must refer to something nearby:

$[_S$ Jane$_i$ saw herself$_{i/*j}]$; $[_S$ Jane$_i$ thinks $[_S$ Tarzan$_k$ saw herself$_{*i/*j}]]$

All of these pronouns position like NPs (not like nouns!).

- Interrogative: *who, what, where*, etc.

These introduce WH questions, and have a "double" positioning; they are overtly sentence- or clause-initial, but they correspond to an empty position (often NP, possibly another type, e.g., PP) somewhere in the clause:

$[_S$ What$_i$ is Mary putting $[_{NP}\emptyset]_i$ in the soup?$]$
$[_S$ Where$_i$ is Mary putting that old shoe $[_{PP}\emptyset]_i$?$]$

- Relative: *which, who, (that), where,* etc.

These introduce relative (adjectival) clauses and also show the "double" positioning just described:

[$_{NP}$ the knife [$_S$ which$_i$ you put [$_{NP}$Ø]$_i$ on the table]] (... is gone.)

- Expletive: *it, there*

There is [$_{NP}$ a letter] on the desk (, isn't there/*it/?)
(cf. Mary is with Max in Belgium, isn't she/*Mary/*he/*it?)

It is raining.
It is obvious [$_S$ that Mary is in Belgium].

These reside in "subject" position, and are grammatical subjects, but have no semantic content. The expletive pronoun *there* "corresponds" to an NP. The expletive pronoun *it* fills the subject of a "weather" sentence, or "corresponds" to a sentence.

Prepositions: *in, at, on, with, by,* etc.

These "license" (usu.) NPs into a sentence which are not already licensed in as a subject or object. Prepositional phrases are often "adjuncts," though they may in certain instances be complements to a verb, e.g.:

Mary saw a book [$_{PP}$ on the desk].(adjunct; cf., "Mary saw a book")
Mary put a book [$_{PP}$ on the desk].(complement; cf., *"Mary put a book")

Prepositions position to the left of NP, at the left periphery of PP.

Conjunctions:

- Coordinating: *and, or (,but)*

These join elements of identical type and status, e.g., NP and NP, N and N, S and S, etc. Such elements are "reversible" around the conjunct (e.g., The book and the pencil/the pencil and the book). These position between the elements joined.

- Subordinating:
  (i) Adverbial subordinating conjunctions: *because, before, after, until,* etc.

These introduce phrases or sentences of lesser status (subordinate/ "embedded") with an "adverbial" function in a larger ("matrix") sentence. These subordinators "move" with the parts that they introduce:

Mary left because she was sleepy.
Because she was sleepy, Mary left.

(ii) Complementizers: (NP function): *that, whether, for (to)*.

These introduce embedded sentences that appear in NP positions such as subject or object. These too move with the sentences that they introduce:

Everyone believes [that Clark is Superman].
[That Clark is Superman] is believed by everyone.
Everyone wonders [whether Zelda is Wonder Woman].
Jane wants very much [for Cheetah to live outdoors].

Appendix 2

Argument Structures

arrive, V, ...,	Args: 1 (tentative)	Cats: NP	Theta roles: experiencer
be, V, ...,	Args: 1 2	Cats: NP NP/AjP/PP	Theta roles: entity quality
believe, V, ...,	Args: 1 2	Cats: NP NP	Theta roles: agent theme
buy, V, ...,	Args: 1 2	Cats: NP NP	Theta roles: agent theme
creep, V, ...,	Args: 1	Cats: NP	Theta roles: agent
eat, V, ...	Args: 1 (2	Cats: NP NP	Theta roles: agent theme)
hear, V, ...	Args: 1 2	Cats: NP NP	Theta roles: experiencer theme

leave, V, ...,	Args:	Cats:	Theta roles:
	1	NP	agent
	(2	NP	theme)
like, V, ...,	Args:	Cats:	Theta roles:
	1	NP	experiencer
	2	NP	theme
(be) likely, Aj, ...,	Args:	Cats:	Theta roles:
	1	–	–
	2	CP(fin)/	theme
		TP(inf)	
mow, V, ...,	Args:	Cats:	Theta roles:
	1	NP	agent
	2	NP	theme
place, V, ...,	Args:	Cats:	Theta roles:
	1	NP	agent
	2	NP	theme
	3	PP	location
play, V, ...,	Args:	Cats:	Theta roles:
	1	NP	agent
	(2	NP	theme)
put, V, ...,	Args:	Cats:	Theta roles:
	1	NP	agent
	2	NP	theme
	3	PP	location
say, V, ...,	Args:	Cats:	Theta roles:
	1	NP	agent
	2	NP/CP	theme
see, V, ...,	Args:	Cats:	Theta roles:
	1	NP	experiencer
	2	NP	theme
seem, V, ...,	Args:	Cats:	Theta roles:
	1	–	–
	2	CP(fin)/	theme
		TP(inf)	
sell, V, ...,	Args:	Cats:	Theta roles:
	1	NP	agent
	2	NP	theme

| *smile*, V, …, | Args: | Cats: | Theta roles: |
| | 1 | NP | agent |

swim, V, …,	Args:	Cats:	Theta roles:
	1	NP	agent
	(2	NP	theme)

take, V, …,	Args:	Cats:	Theta roles:
	1	NP	agent
	2	NP	theme

tell, V, …,	Args:	Cats:	Theta roles:
	1	NP	agent
	2	NP	goal
	3	NP	theme

visit, V, …,	Args:	Cats:	Theta roles:
	1	NP	agent
	2	NP	theme

want, V, …,	Args:	Cats:	Theta roles:
	1	NP	experiencer
	2	NP	theme

wash, V, …,	Args:	Cats:	Theta roles:
	1	NP	agent
	2	NP	theme

watch, V, …,	Args:	Cats:	Theta roles:
	1	NP	agent
	2	NP	theme

water, V, …,	Args:	Cats:	Theta roles:
	1	NP	agent
	2	NP	theme

win, V, …,	Args:	Cats:	Theta roles:
	1	NP	experiencer
	2	NP	theme

Index